FITWAFFLE'S
Easy Air Fryer

100 *of* my BEST BAKES, QUICK DESSERTS *and* SIMPLE MEALS

Eloise Head

EBURY PRESS

Welcome

Contents

ABOUT THIS BOOK	7
ABOUT ME	8
LET'S TALK ABOUT AIR FRYERS	10
BREAKFAST and BRUNCH	20
SNACKING and SIDES	56
SPEEDY LUNCHES	96
EASY DINNERS	122
BROWNIES, BLONDIES and COOKIES	152
CAKES, CRUMBLES and PASTRY	180
SEASONAL	218
INDEX	248
CONVERSION TABLES	252
ACKNOWLEDGEMENTS	254

ABOUT THIS BOOK

I can't believe I'm writing a fourth book! I know I say this every time, but I really am continuously blown away by all your love and support. Thank you from the bottom of my heart, it means so much to me.

I'm really, really excited to bring you this book. I'm receiving more and more air fryer recipe requests, so this was definitely a difficult one to keep a secret.

In true Fitwaffle-style, all the recipes are fuss-free, easy and delicious with accessible ingredients that you'll find at the supermarket, because if you're like me, you probably don't want to visit three different shops looking for twenty different ingredients to make one recipe.

Cooking in the air fryer is something I've fallen in love with because it's just so quick and easy! I genuinely get excited at the thought that I don't have to turn on my oven and wait 15 minutes for it to preheat to make a meal – I can just whack it in the air fryer and save time and energy.

One of the reasons I'm so excited about this book, is that it doesn't just contain sweet recipes, 50 per cent of the recipes are savoury! Something that you guys are always asking for is more savoury recipes, so I hope you'll love these as much as I do. Some recipes are fan favourites that you'll find on my social media, the rest are brand new and exclusive to the book.

You'll find everything from breakfast and brunch, snacks and sides, speedy lunches and easy dinners, to brownies, blondies and cookies, cakes, crumbles and pastries, and of course we can't forget the fun seasonal recipes too.

A lot of the sweet recipes are 'small batch', meaning they'll fit inside the air fryer all at once, rather than cooking in multiple batches. You'll find cakes and crumbles for two, small trays of brownies and blondies for six, and lots of cookie recipes using a small batch of dough.

This air fryer book is perfect for beginners; whether you're new to cooking and baking or just want to try something different, there's something in here for everyone.

I can't wait for you to get started with this book. I hope it brings you joy, inspiration and of course ... delicious food.

Enjoy!

ABOUT ME

Hi, I'm Eloise, best known online as Fitwaffle. I'm a recipe developer, content creator, bestselling author, all-round foodie and former fitness professional.

One of my most frequently asked questions is 'What does Fitwaffle mean?' So let me give you a quick backstory.

I came up with the name about eight years ago when I was working full time as a personal trainer and gym manager. I was learning to enjoy all foods in moderation after a previously poor relationship with food. I'm a big believer in viewing health as an overall lifestyle, both physically and mentally, enjoying all foods in moderation and not demonising specific foods.

Fitwaffle encompasses my two passions, fitness and food. The 'fit' part also means fitting all foods into your diet, and the 'waffle' part also refers to 'waffling on', because I tend to talk a lot ...

Food has always been a big part of my life. I used to bake with my great auntie when I was little. I think this is where my love of cooking started. We always had so much fun making biscuits, cakes and everything and anything with pastry. She also made the best roast potatoes I've ever eaten!

It's my personal mission to help others learn to enjoy all foods in moderation and improve their relationship with food. It's also my goal to help people become more confident in the kitchen, by showing that baking and cooking don't have to be intimidating, making it easy and accessible for people of all ages and skill levels.

So that's me in a nutshell, let's dive into the book!

SO LET'S TALK ABOUT AIR FRYERS

HOW DO THEY WORK?

Air fryers work by circulating hot air around the food, similar to a convection oven. This process cooks the outside of the food first, creating a crispy, brown coating while keeping the inside soft. We can adjust the temperature to play around with this, like in baking for example.

ALL AIR FRYERS ARE DIFFERENT – GETTING TO KNOW YOURS

I've tested these recipes in a range of air fryers to make sure they work properly, and surprise surprise, the food cooks slightly differently in each one. Not exactly what you want to hear, but don't worry, it's all about getting to know your specific air fryer, so here are some tips:

- **The power of your air fryer:** It's a good idea to make a note of the wattage of your air fryer, as the amount of power it has will affect how the food cooks. You can find this by looking at the label, the booklet that came with your air fryer or on the manufacturer's website.

  Just like ovens, some air fryers run hotter and some run colder. It's a great idea to buy an oven thermometer to check the actual heat of your air fryer. If you find your air fryer runs hotter or colder than the temperature displayed, you can adjust the temperature of your air fryer up or down accordingly.

- **Check if the food is done:** You will notice throughout the book I have written cues so you know when the food is done. For meat, you can use a probe thermometer, for cakes you can use a toothpick, for potatoes and veggies you can use the fork test – if a fork goes in easily, it's tender and ready to eat. Other cues are more visual, for example the colour of the food, but remember, the heat comes from the top, so just because it looks done on the top, that doesn't mean it's done in the middle or the bottom – this is especially important when it comes to baking.

The more you cook and use your air fryer, the better you will get at knowing exactly when your food is done and cooked to your liking.

To check your food, it's really easy just to open the air fryer door and have a peek to see how it's getting on. Remember, you can always add time, but you can't take it away, so when you're learning your air fryer, it's better to check your food a few times than burn it.

TYPE

All these recipes will work whether you have an air fryer with a basket (or two), one that looks like a mini oven with racks, or a halogen air fryer. Here's some adjustment you may need to make:

- **Air fryer ovens:** The top rack is always the hottest, just like in a regular oven. For best results, I would recommend placing the food on the middle rack of the air fryer and cooking one rack at a time, rather than stacking them on top of each other.

- **Halogen air fryers:** These often cook slower, so will need approximately 30 per cent extra cooking time.

SIZE

I would always recommend getting a larger air fryer rather than a smaller one. I have two at home, one is a 5.5-litre basket air fryer, and the other is an 11-litre oven-style air fryer, and I love them both. The first air fryer I ever bought was 3.8 litres and it was just far too small, even for a two-person household.

The most popular air fryer type is a basket/drawer air fryer, so these recipes have been written with this in mind, but they can easily be adjusted to suit any air fryer, you just may need an extra piece of equipment for the occasional recipe.

I've made sure to stick to equipment and recipe sizes that will work in most air fryers. Head to the special equipment section on page 16 to find out more.

BUTTONS/FUNCTIONS

For each recipe, I give you the time and temperature to set your air fryer to. This is for the standard 'air fry' setting. For most air fryers, you can just set the time and temperature and you're ready to go.

DO YOU NEED TO PREHEAT YOUR AIR FRYER?

The short answer is yes. Just like a regular oven, your food will cook better and more consistently when your air fryer has been preheated. This is especially important when it comes to baking, as the food needs to go in at the right temperature. As you get to know your air fryer, you may find that for some recipes preheating is not necessary, as your air fryer heats up really quickly and it's hotter than the average air fryer.

Some air fryers have a preheat function which will beep when the temperature is reached. If your air fryer doesn't have this, just set it to the required temperature and let it heat up for 3–4 minutes.

OVEN TIMES VS AIR FRYER COOKING TIMES

Almost anything you can cook in the oven can also be cooked in the air fryer, there just need to be some adjustments made. Here are some easy charts to help you convert oven cooking times and temperatures to air fryer cooking times and temperatures.

AIR FRYER COOKING TIME	OVEN COOKING TIME
8 minutes	10 minutes
12 minutes	15 minutes
16 minutes	20 minutes
20 minutes	25 minutes
24 minutes	30 minutes
28 minutes	35 minutes
32 minutes	40 minutes
36 minutes	45 minutes
40 minutes	50 minutes

AIR FRYER TEMPERATURE	OVEN COOKING TEMPERATURE
140°C (275°F)	180°C (160°C fan)/ 350°F/Gas Mark 4
150°C (300°F)	190°C (170°C fan)/ 375°F/Gas Mark 5
160°C (325°F)	200°C (180°C fan)/ 400°F/Gas Mark 6
170°C (340°F)	210°C (190°C fan)/ 410°F/Gas Mark 6½
180°C (350°F)	220°C (200°C fan)/ 425°F/Gas Mark 7
190°C (375°F)	230°C (210°C fan)/ 450°F/Gas Mark 8
200°C (400°F)	240°C (220°C fan)/ 475°F/Gas Mark 9

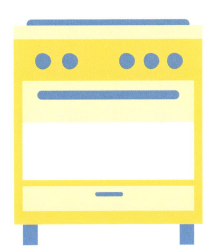

TIPS and TRICKS

1
OVERCROWDING

The hot air needs to circulate freely around the food, so overcrowding the air fryer or piling up the food will mean it cooks slower. This also applies to baking – using a tin or dish that is too close to the edge of the air fryer won't allow the air to circulate freely.

2
WHAT WENT WRONG?

Let's not beat around the bush, you may not get it right first time. Usually if something goes wrong, it's because the food was cooked at the incorrect temperature or not using the right equipment. Especially when it comes to baking, make sure you follow the ingredients list and instructions perfectly for best results.

3
METRIC VS IMPERIAL MEASUREMENTS

You'll find both in this book for my friends across the pond. My preference is to use a food scale, especially for baking where accuracy is key for consistent bakes. When referring to teaspoons and tablespoons, these are all level, unless specified. You'll be surprised how much extra you can add by using a heaped spoon by accident.

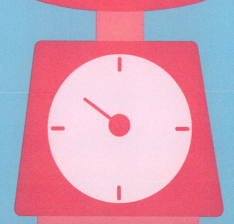

4 EXPERIMENT

The best way to learn your air fryer and to become more confident using it is just to use it more frequently. Use the conversion charts on pages 12–13 and try using it to cook things you would usually cook in your oven.

5 OIL/COOKING SPRAY

My preference is extra virgin olive oil for taste and crispiness. You can buy your own spray bottle and decant the oil into it. Oil can be sprayed directly into the air fryer to stop food from sticking, and directly onto the food to help crisp it up. I wouldn't recommend using low-calorie oil sprays, as these can damage your air fryer over time.

6 CLEANING

It's best to clean your air fryer after every use. Air fryers are generally quick and easy to clean with some soapy water and a rinse afterwards. If you don't clean your air fryer, you may find it gets smoky the next time you use it, and the flavours and smells can transfer to other foods.

AIR FRYER SPECIAL EQUIPMENT

I'm sure most of you don't want to go out and buy lots of new equipment to start cooking in your air fryer, so I've tried to keep the 'special equipment' to a minumum and reuse the same equipment throughout the book. These are all written clearly on each recipe.

1 **Silicone air fryer liners/dishes:** Silicone is easy to clean, nonstick and so versatile. I would recommend getting a silicone dish with handles that fits inside your air fryer so it's easy to remove. Silicone cupcake/muffin cases are also great, as they will hold their shape when baking, they're less likely to blow around and they're reusable – I use them a few times throughout this book.

2 **Traditional bakeware:** Any material that can go in the oven can also go in the air fryer, it just depends on the size. For example, 15cm (6in) round cake tins will work great in the air fryer, but you may need to buy a slightly smaller loaf tin if yours is too big to fit inside the air fryer. Individual pudding tins are also great for making Yorkshire puddings.

3 **Thick baking paper:** As we know, things can blow around a bit in the air fryer, so using a thicker baking paper (such as BacoFoil non-stick baking paper) or folding it up can stop it moving around and messing up your food. You can also secure it with clips or weigh it down.

4 **15cm (6in) square tins:** The majority of my tray bakes in this book are baked in a 15cm (6in) square metal tin. This size will fit in the majority of air fryers, but you can always use a metal tin of a different shape if you prefer. For example, the area of a 15cm x 15cm (6in x 6in) tin is 225cm (36in), so a tin that is 18cm x 13cm (7in x 5in) will also be fine as the area is 234cm (35in), so you won't need to make any large adjustments. Be careful using a dish that is much smaller or larger, or of a different material such as ceramic or glass, as the bake will cook differently and will need adjusting. I would recommend getting the exact equipment stated in the recipe when baking.

5 **Thermometers:** These are your best friend for finding out how hot your air fryer is and checking if your food is cooked through. You can get oven thermometers and meat probe thermometers to ensure everything is cooking how it should be.

6 **Ramekins:** I absolutely love using ceramic ramekins in the air fryer. The ones I generally use are 6cm x 6cm (2½in x 2½in) (width x height), unless stated otherwise.

7 **Spray bottle:** These are super handy for filling with oil to spray your air fryer and food. I use mine all the time, not just for the air fryer, but for spraying tins too.

INGREDIENTS TIPS and TRICKS

Eggs

You'll notice in a few recipes in this book I use half an egg. This is because a small egg was still too big, and I wanted to make the recipe fit nicely into the air fryer without baking in multiple batches. To halve an egg accurately, place a bowl or ramekin on a food scale, crack in the egg and lightly beat it, then remove half the egg according to the weight. You can store the remaining half of the egg in the refrigerator and use it in another recipe or have it in your breakfast the next day. Alternatively, if you wanted to use the whole egg and cook in batches, you can double the recipe ingredients accordingly.

Sprinkles

In recipes that use sprinkles in the cake batter, for example the Funfetti Cake on page 184, I would recommend using high-quality sprinkles. Some sprinkles lose their colour very easily and will turn your cake batter a greeny-blue colour.

Melting chocolate

It's easiest to do this in the microwave or using a double boiler. First, break the chocolate into about 1cm (½in) pieces.

In the microwave

Put the chocolate pieces into a microwave-safe bowl and microwave on a medium setting in 30-second bursts, stirring at each interval. When the chocolate has almost fully melted, continue to stir it with a spoon until all the lumps have disappeared and the chocolate is runny and smooth.

In a double boiler

Make sure you have a saucepan and a large heatproof bowl (I recommend glass) that sits about halfway into your pan. Fill the saucepan with about 5cm (2in) of water. Put your chocolate pieces into the bowl, then sit it on top of the saucepan and turn on the heat so the water starts to simmer. As the water heats up and steam is released, the steam stays trapped between the bowl and the pan, which then heats and melts the chocolate. As this happens, gently stir the chocolate until it's runny and smooth.

Recipes

Veggie Breakfast Burrito	24
Egg, Bean & Cheese Breakfast Pot	26
Loaded Hash Browns	28
Shakshuka	31
Savoury French Toast Bake	32
Sausage & Bacon French Toast Rolls	34
Bacon & Cheese Quesadilla	36
Speculoos French Toast Bake	39
Blueberry Pancakes	40
Choc Chip Cookie Baked Oats	42
Stuffed Brioche French Toast	44
Cinnamon Roll Granola	47
Upside Down Apple Danish	48
French Toast Bites	50
Cinnamon Pastry Swirls	52
Chocolate Toast Pies	55

I DO LOVE BREAKFAST!

As you may already guess, I'm usually a sweet breakfast kinda gal, but my husband loves a savoury breakfast – everything eggs and hash browns and baked beans – so we have the best of both worlds in this chapter, from a Bacon and Cheese Quesadilla and Loaded Hash Browns, to Stuffed Brioche French Toast and Cinnamon Roll Granola. Also, who says breakfast has to be eaten in the morning … these recipes are perfect for any time of the day.

Sweet ...

or savoury?

VEGGIE BREAKFAST BURRITO

Makes 1

A breakfast burrito is such a delicious way to start the day. Scrambled eggs, cheese and your favourite fillings, all wrapped in a warm, toasted tortilla. It's hearty and so customisable to suit your taste.

15 minutes

SPECIAL EQUIPMENT:
Air fryer-safe dish

2 large eggs
10g (0.5oz) butter, melted
40ml (3 tbsp) milk or cream
1 large tortilla
A handful of grated cheese of your choice (I use Cheddar and Red Leicester)
½ avocado, sliced
1 medium tomato, diced
1–2 tsp chopped fresh chives
Olive oil spray
Salt and pepper
Your favourite sauce, to serve

01 Preheat the air fryer to 150°C (300°F).

02 In the dish, whisk together the eggs, melted butter, milk or cream and some salt and pepper.

03 Place the dish in the air fryer and cook for 2 minutes. Gently stir your eggs, then cook again for 2 minutes. Keep doing this until the eggs are almost cooked to your liking. Remember they will continue to cook when toasting the burrito. Remove from the air fryer.

04 Lay your tortilla on a flat surface, scoop the eggs into the middle, sprinkle over the cheese, then place the sliced avocado on top. Scatter over the diced tomato and chopped chives. Wrap the burrito up by folding in the sides, then tightly rolling it up from the bottom.

05 Spray the air fryer rack or basket with oil, then place the burrito on the rack or in the basket with the fold at the base so it doesn't unravel, and spray the top with oil.

06 Air fry at 200°C (400°F) for 5 minutes, or until it's crisp and golden. Cut in half and serve with your favourite sauce. Enjoy!

For extra flavour add the sauce from page 136).

EGG, BEAN and CHEESE BREAKFAST POT

Serves 1

This is one of my go-to cosy breakfasts. It's so simple to make and packed with flavour – egg, mushroom, tomatoes, baked beans and cheese all baked together.

15 minutes

SPECIAL EQUIPMENT:
Large (10cm x 5cm/4in x 2in) air fryer-safe ramekin

1 mushroom, sliced (optional)
2 cherry tomatoes, cut in half
3 tbsp baked beans
1 medium egg
10g (0.5oz) cheese of your choice, grated
Salt and pepper

01 Preheat the air fryer to 200°C (400°F).

02 If using, place the mushroom on the air fryer rack or in the basket and air fry for 5 minutes.

03 Remove the mushroom from the air fryer and transfer into the ramekin. Add the tomatoes, scoop the beans on top, then make a well in the middle with a spoon and crack the egg in. Season with salt and pepper and sprinkle the cheese on top.

04 Put the ramekin into the air fryer and air fry at 180°C (350°F) for 5–6 minutes until the egg is cooked to your liking. Leave to cool for a few minutes, as it will be very hot, then remove from the air fryer and enjoy!

LOADED HASH BROWNS

Makes 4

Loaded hash browns are the ultimate comfort breakfast. Crispy potatoes, topped with chives, sour cream and crispy bacon bits. They're super easy and delicious, and perfect for any time of the day, not just for breakfast.

30 minutes + 10 minutes soaking

2 large floury potatoes (I use Maris Piper)
1 small/medium egg, beaten
1 tsp cornflour (cornstarch)
Olive oil spray
40g (1.5oz) cheese, grated
Salt and pepper

FOR THE TOPPINGS:
Sour cream
Chopped fresh chives
Cooked crumbled bacon bits

01 Peel and coarsely grate your potatoes. Then soak in a medium–large bowl of cold water for 10 minutes.

02 Drain the grated potato. Dry it in a clean cloth or tea towel, squeezing to remove the excess water, then return to the bowl.

03 Add the egg, cornflour (cornstarch) and some salt and pepper and mix it all together.

04 Preheat the air fryer to 200°C (400°F).

05 Spray the air fryer rack or basket with oil and divide the mixture into 4 equal patties. Place in the air fryer and spray with oil again. Cook for 14–15 minutes until crisp and golden.

06 Sprinkle the grated cheese on top, then air fry again for 2–3 minutes until the cheese has melted.

FOR THE TOPPINGS:
07 Dollop on your favourite toppings. I used sour cream, fresh chives and cooked crumbled bacon bits. Serve straight away and enjoy!

SHAKSHUKA

Serves 1-2

This shakshuka is super quick and easy to make, and it's so satisfying. Poached eggs in a rich tomato sauce spiced with cumin and paprika. I love serving it with crusty bread to soak up every bit of deliciousness and it's perfect for breakfast, lunch or dinner.

25 minutes

SPECIAL EQUIPMENT:
Air fryer-safe dish

200g (7oz) canned chopped tomatoes
½ red (bell) pepper, deseeded and finely diced
1 tsp paprika
1 tsp ground cumin
1 tsp chilli flakes (optional)
1 garlic clove, minced
2 small/medium eggs
1 tbsp chopped fresh coriander (cilantro)
2 tbsp crumbled feta
Salt and pepper

01 Preheat the air fryer to 180°C (350°F).

02 In the dish, stir together the chopped tomatoes, diced (bell) pepper, paprika, cumin, chilli flakes, if using, minced garlic and some salt and pepper until combined. Air fry for 10 minutes.

03 Carefully remove the dish from the air fryer then, using a spoon, create 2 wells in the tomato mixture and crack an egg into each well.

04 Air fry again for 10 minutes, or until the eggs are cooked to your liking.

05 Sprinkle with the coriander (cilantro) and feta and serve. Enjoy!

SAVOURY FRENCH TOAST BAKE

Serves 2

This is the perfect 'make-ahead' breakfast, it's easy to prepare the night before, then just add the toppings and bake the next day. It's hearty, filling and delicious and ideal for sharing.

30 minutes + overnight soaking

SPECIAL EQUIPMENT:
15cm x 15cm (6in x 6in) air fryer-safe dish (or one of a similar size that fits inside your air fryer)

3 slices of bread
2 large eggs
125ml (½ cup) milk of your choice
200g (7oz) baked beans
50g (1.75oz) Cheddar and/or mozzarella, grated
Salt and pepper

01 Cut the bread into 2.5cm (1in) cubes, keeping the crusts on or cutting them off (I usually leave them on). Set aside.

02 In a medium–large bowl, mix together the eggs with the milk and some salt and pepper until combined. Add the bread and mix together, using a wooden spoon or rubber spatula, until the cubes are all fully coated.

03 Transfer the bread and any remaining mixture to the dish. Cover it with cling film (plastic wrap), then leave to soak in the refrigerator overnight.

04 The next day, remove the cling film, cover the dish with foil and preheat the air fryer to 160°C (325°F).

05 Place the dish in the air fryer and cook for 15–17 minutes.

06 Remove from the air fryer and take off the foil, then pour the baked beans on top and sprinkle over the cheese, then air fry for a further 10 minutes, or until the cheese has melted and the beans are hot. Leave to cool for about 5 minutes, then serve warm. Enjoy!

SAUSAGE and BACON FRENCH TOAST ROLLS

Makes 6

These are such a fun and delicious breakfast, especially for kids … or adults, no judgement! Just cook your fillings and roll up them in a slice of bread and cook until golden. They're super easy and customisable.

30 minutes

- 6 thin sausages (I use Richmond skinless)
- 3 rashers of streaky bacon
- 6 slices of soft bread, crusts removed
- 1 large egg
- 60ml (¼ cup) milk of your choice
- 6 slices of American cheese
- Olive oil spray
- Salt and pepper
- Your favourite sauce, to serve

01   Preheat the air fryer to 200°C (400°F).

02   Place your sausages in the air fryer and air fry for 4 minutes, then add your bacon and continue to air fry for 6–7 minutes until they're both cooked through. If you like your bacon extra crispy, add it to the air fryer earlier.

03   Roll the slices of bread out nice and flat with a rolling pin.

04   In a small–medium bowl, whisk together the egg, milk and some salt and pepper until combined and set aside.

05   Cut each rasher of bacon in half so it's roughly the same length as the sausage, then place 1 slice of cheese, half a rasher of bacon and 1 cooked sausage at the short edge closest to you on a slice of bread, then tightly roll it up. Secure with a toothpick if needed. Repeat to make another 5 rolls.

06   Spray your air fryer rack or basket with oil, then dip the rolls in the egg mixture, dripping off any excess (you don't need to soak them). Place them directly in your air fryer and spray again with oil.

07   Cook for 5–7 minutes until the bread is golden brown.

08   Serve straight away with your favourite sauce. Enjoy!

BACON and CHEESE QUESADILLA

Serves 1-2

This is one of my favourite breakfasts. It's so easy to make, packed with scrambled eggs, cheese, bacon and your favourite toppings, all melted inside a crispy tortilla. Yum!

20 minutes

SPECIAL EQUIPMENT:
Air fryer-safe dish

- 2 rashers of streaky bacon
- 2 large eggs
- 10g (0.5 oz) butter, melted
- 40ml (3 tbsp) milk or cream
- Olive oil spray
- 2 medium-large tortillas (make sure they fit in your air fryer)
- 1-2 tsp chopped fresh chives
- 1 medium tomato, diced
- A handful of grated cheese of your choice (I use Cheddar and Red Leicester)
- Salt and pepper
- Your favourite sauce, to serve

01 Preheat the air fryer to 200°C (400°F).

02 Place your bacon on the air fryer rack or in the basket and cook for 6 minutes, or until cooked to your liking. Chop the bacon into little pieces and set aside.

03 In the dish, whisk together the eggs, melted butter, milk or cream and some salt and pepper.

04 Place the dish in the air fryer and cook at 150°C (300°F) for 2 minutes. Gently stir your eggs, then cook again for 2 minutes. Keep doing this until the eggs are almost cooked to your liking. Remember the eggs will continue to cook when toasting the tortilla. Remove the eggs from the air fryer.

05 Spray the air fryer rack or basket with oil, then place 1 tortilla on the rack or in the basket. Scoop the eggs on top, then scatter over the chopped bacon, sprinkle with the chopped chives and diced tomato, then sprinkle over the cheese.

06 Place the remaining tortilla on top and press down so it sticks, then spray it with oil and air fry at 200°C (400°F) for 4–5 minutes until the cheese has melted and the tortilla is golden.

07 Remove from the air fryer, cut into triangles and dip in your favourite sauce. Enjoy!

SPECULOOS FRENCH TOAST BAKE

Serves 2

If you love speculoos (cookie butter), this recipe is for you. It's loaded with cinnamon, vanilla, brown sugar and speculoos spread. It's easy to make ahead, absolutely delicious and perfect for sharing.

40 minutes + overnight soaking

SPECIAL EQUIPMENT:
15cm x 15cm (6in x 6in) baking tin (or one of a similar size that fits inside your air fryer)

- 3 thick slices of the white bread of your choice
- 2 large eggs
- 125ml (½ cup) milk of your choice
- 1 tsp ground cinnamon
- ½ tsp vanilla extract
- 1 tbsp light brown sugar
- 30g (2 tbsp) speculoos spread (cookie butter) (I use Biscoff), melted

01 Cut the bread into 2.5cm (1in) cubes, keeping the crusts on or cutting them off (I usually leave them on). Set aside.

02 In a medium-large bowl, mix together the eggs, milk, cinnamon, vanilla extract and light brown sugar until combined. Add the bread and mix together using a wooden spoon or rubber spatula until the cubes are all fully coated.

03 Transfer the bread and any remaining mixture to the tin. Cover it with cling film (plastic wrap), then leave to soak in the refrigerator overnight.

04 The next day, remove the cling film and cover with foil. Preheat the air fryer to 160°C (325°F).

05 Place the tin in the air fryer and bake for 15–17 minutes. Remove from the air fryer and take off the foil, then continue to bake for a further 10–12 minutes until a knife comes out clean. Leave to cool for about 5 minutes.

06 Drizzle the melted speculoos spread (cookie butter) all over the top and serve warm. Enjoy!

07 Store in an airtight container in the refrigerator for up to 2 days. You can reheat it in the air fryer for 3–4 minutes, or until hot throughout.

BLUEBERRY PANCAKES

Makes 6

These pancakes are super thick and fluffy and so easy to make. They're bursting with sweet, juicy blueberries, and they're absolutely delicious. Perfect for a cosy weekend morning ... or whenever you fancy pancakes.

20 minutes + 15 minutes resting

SPECIAL EQUIPMENT:
Six 10cm (4in) silicone moulds

80g (5 tbsp) full-fat (5%) Greek yogurt
150ml (⅔ cup) semi-skimmed or skimmed milk
1 medium egg
15g (0.75oz) salted butter, melted
1 tbsp maple syrup
120g (scant ¾ cup) plain (all-purpose) flour
1 tbsp caster sugar
½ tsp baking powder
½ tsp bicarbonate of soda
Good pinch of salt
100g (3.5oz) fresh blueberries
Cooking oil spray

TO SERVE (OPTIONAL):
Fresh berries
Whipped cream
Maple syrup, for drizzling

01 In a large bowl, using a balloon whisk, mix together the Greek yogurt and milk until combined, then add the egg, melted butter and maple syrup and whisk until smooth.

02 Add all the dry ingredients and fold in until smooth and lump-free, then fold in the blueberries. Leave the batter to rest for 15 minutes.

03 Preheat the air fryer to 160°C (320°F).

04 Spray the silicone moulds with oil making sure the base and edges are coated so the pancakes don't stick.

05 Scoop half a cup of batter into each mould and smooth it out evenly.

06 Air fry for 8-10 minutes, then carefully flip them over out of their moulds and cook for another 3-4 minutes until golden brown and cooked through.

TO SERVE (OPTIONAL):
07 Serve straight away with your favourite toppings, if using. I love to use berries, whipped cream and maple syrup. Enjoy!

CHOC CHIP COOKIE BAKED OATS

Makes 1

Baked oats that taste like cookies – a dream come true. These oats are so easy to make, packed with basic ingredients that you may already have in your cupboard. The batter is super versatile so you can mix up the flavours too ... why not swap the chocolate chips for blueberries?

30 minutes

SPECIAL EQUIPMENT:
6cm x 6cm (2½in x 2½in) air fryer-safe ramekin

45g (⅔ cup) rolled oats
60g (4 tbsp) Greek or plain yogurt or 75g (2.5oz) mashed banana
25ml (2 tbsp) honey or maple syrup
10g (0.5 oz) butter, melted and cooled slightly (optional)
60ml (¼ cup) milk of your choice
¼ tsp vanilla extract
⅛ tsp salt
20g (1½ tbsp) chocolate chips + extra for sprinkling

01 Preheat the air fryer to 170°C (340°F).

02 Put the oats, yogurt or mashed banana, honey or maple syrup, melted butter, if using, milk, vanilla extract and salt into a small bowl and stir until everything is combined, then fold in the chocolate chips.

03 Pour the mixture into the ramekin and sprinkle more chocolate chips on top.

04 Place the ramekin in the air fryer and air fry for 20–25 minutes until cooked through. The time will vary depending on the size and shape of your ramekin.

05 Leave to stand for a few minutes before removing from the air fryer. Be careful as the ramekin will be very hot! Grab a spoon and enjoy.

Feel free to swap the chocolate chips for blueberries, raspberries or whatever you wish.

STUFFED BRIOCHE FRENCH TOAST

Makes 1

This is like eating dessert for breakfast and if you love a sweet breakfast, this one is for you. Stuff thick brioche bread with your chosen filling – I like chocolate or chocolate spread – dip it in egg and cook to perfection. So easy and so delicious – your mornings will never be the same again.

20 minutes

- 1 x 5cm (2in)-thick slice of brioche bread
- Filling of your choice (I like to use a square or 2 of chocolate or pipe in some chocolate spread. You could also use another spread or even some fruit)
- 1 medium egg
- 80ml (⅓ cup) milk of your choice
- 1 tsp vanilla extract
- ½ tsp ground cinnamon

TO SERVE (OPTIONAL):
- Icing (powdered) sugar, for dusting
- Maple syrup or chocolate spread, for drizzling

01 With a knife, make a small incision about three quarters of the way in on one side of the bread to make a pocket. Insert your filling into the pocket.

02 Preheat the air fryer to 160°C (325°F).

03 In a medium–large bowl, mix together the egg, milk, vanilla extract and cinnamon, using a whisk or fork, until combined, then dunk in the bread, making sure it's fully coated. Let it sit for a couple of minutes, then turn it over and repeat until most of the mixture has been soaked up.

04 Feel free to line the air fryer rack or basket with thick baking paper so the bread doesn't stick. Place the bread in the air fryer and cook for 12–15 minutes, turning it over halfway through, until it's crisp and golden and the outside is firm to touch.

TO SERVE (OPTIONAL):

05 Dust with icing (powdered) sugar and drizzle with maple syrup or chocolate spread, if you wish. Enjoy!

CINNAMON ROLL GRANOLA

Makes approx. 350g (12.4oz)

I absolutely love granola – sprinkling it on yogurt or just having it with milk. Cinnamon rolls are one of my favourite desserts, so this was a no-brainer – a mixture of oats, puffed rice cereal, vanilla extract, brown sugar and cinnamon. It's the granola of dreams.

20 minutes

- 100ml (scant ½ cup) honey or maple syrup
- 1 tsp vanilla extract
- 30ml (1½ tbsp) vegetable oil or coconut oil
- 130g (1⅓ cups) rolled oats
- 65g (2½ cups) puffed rice cereal
- 2 tbsp light brown sugar
- 1 tbsp ground cinnamon
- ¼ tsp salt

01 Preheat the air fryer to 160°C (325°F).

02 In a medium bowl, mix together the honey or maple syrup, vanilla extract and oil until combined.

03 Fold in the oats, puffed rice cereal, light brown sugar, cinnamon and salt until fully combined.

04 Line the air fryer rack or basket with a sheet of thick baking paper. Pour the mixture onto the baking paper and spread it out evenly.

05 Air fry for 11–13 minutes, stirring every 4 minutes, until toasted and golden.

06 Remove from the air fryer and spread it out on a baking tray to cool. Break up any large chunks.

07 Store in an airtight container at room temperature for up to 1 month. Enjoy!

You can add pumpkin seeds, pecans, almonds, cranberries or really anything you fancy.

UPSIDE DOWN APPLE DANISH

Makes 6

You've probably seen these all over the internet, and for good reason – they're delicious and so easy to make. They're perfect for a fun weekend brunch, after-dinner dessert or afternoon snack.

20 minutes

- 1 sheet ready-rolled puff pastry
- 1 medium apple (I use Granny Smith)
- 6 tbsp honey
- 1 small egg + 1 tsp milk or water, for the egg wash

01 Unravel the puff pastry and cut into 6 even rectangles with a knife or pizza cutter. Tip: lay the pastry in a portrait position, slice vertically down the middle, then horizontally into thirds.

02 Thinly slice the apple. You can keep the skin on or remove it, I usually leave it on.

03 Line the air fryer with a sheet of thick baking paper. The amount of Danishes you can bake at once will depend on the size of your air fryer basket/rack.

04 To make each Danish, drizzle a line of honey about 7.5cm (3in) long onto the baking paper and spread it out slightly with the back of a spoon. Place about 5 apple slices on top of the honey so they overlap slightly, then drizzle them with a little more honey.

05 Place a pastry rectangle on top so the apples are in the middle, then press down gently around the apple with your fingers.

06 In a small bowl, beat the egg and milk or water together to make the egg wash, then brush it over the top of the pastry with a pastry brush.

07 Air fry at 180°C (350°F) for 10–12 minutes until crisp, puffed and golden brown, then leave them to cool slightly.

08 Once cool to touch, gently turn them over to reveal the sweet, sticky honey apples, and they're ready to eat. Enjoy!

Feel free to swap the apple for a couple of fresh peaches to make peach Danishes.

FRENCH TOAST BITES

Serves 1-2

French toast bites are my go-to if I have any leftover buns in the house. They make perfect soft, pillowy French toast and it's so quick and easy to make. Add your choice of toppings and dip them in your favourite sauces.

15 minutes

2 buns of your choice
1 medium egg
60ml (¼ cup) milk of your choice
1 tsp vanilla extract

TO SERVE (OPTIONAL):
Icing (powdered) sugar, for dusting
Maple syrup, for drizzling/dipping

01 Preheat the air fryer to 160°C (325°F).

02 Slice the buns into about 2.5cm (1in) chunks. The number of chunks you end up with will depend on the size of your buns.

03 In a medium bowl, mix together the egg, milk and vanilla extract, using a whisk or fork, until combined, then dunk the chunks of bread, making sure they're fully coated. You don't need to soak them.

04 Feel free to line the air fryer rack or basket with thick baking paper so the bread doesn't stick. Place the bread chunks in your air fryer and air fry for 8 minutes, turning them over halfway through, until they're crisp and golden.

TO SERVE (OPTIONAL):
05 Dust with icing (powdered) sugar and drizzle with/dip in maple syrup, if you wish.

To make these savoury, skip the vanilla extract and swap the icing (powdered) sugar and maple syrup for savoury toppings.

CINNAMON PASTRY SWIRLS

Makes 5

These cinnamon pastry swirls are so nostalgic, so cinnamony and so delicious. Crisp, light, flaky pastry with a buttery cinnamon filling, sprinkled with sugar. Perfect with a cup of tea or coffee.

25 minutes

- 30g (1.25oz) unsalted butter, softened
- 3 tbsp light brown sugar (dark is also fine)
- 1 tsp ground cinnamon
- 1 sheet ready-rolled puff pastry
- 1 small egg + 1 tsp milk or water, for the egg wash
- Granulated sugar, to sprinkle (optional)

01 In a small bowl, mix together the butter, light brown sugar and cinnamon with a fork or spoon to make a paste.

02 Unravel the puff pastry and lay it out in a landscape position, then spread the cinnamon butter over the right half of the pastry and fold the pastry over the cinnamon butter, like you're closing a book.

03 Slice the pastry vertically into 5 strips, then slice each strip vertically in half again, leaving just the tops still connected.

04 Twist the two branches of a strip around each other, then curl into a swirl shape and tuck the end underneath, squeezing it together gently so it doesn't unravel. Repeat to make the remaining swirls.

05 In a small bowl, beat the egg and milk or water together to make the egg wash.

06 Preheat the air fryer to 160°C (325°F).

07 Line the air fryer rack or basket with a sheet of thick baking paper. Place your swirls in the air fryer at least 5cm (2in) apart, then brush with the egg wash and sprinkle with granulated sugar, if using.

08 Air fry for 13–15 minutes until golden brown on top. Leave to cool slightly and they're ready to eat. Enjoy!

Feel free to swap the cinnamon butter for chocolate hazelnut or another spread.

CHOCOLATE TOAST PIES

Makes 3

These are my secret weapon for pleasing anyone who loves chocolate. They're delicious at any time of the day and they're so quick and easy to make with just 2 main ingredients: chocolate spread and bread.

15 minutes

- 3 slices of soft bread
- 3 tsp chocolate hazelnut spread (I use Nutella) + extra, melted, to drizzle (optional)
- 1 small egg + 1 tsp milk or water, for the egg wash
- Icing (powdered) sugar, for dusting (optional)
- Fresh raspberries, to serve (optional)

01 Preheat the air fryer to 180°C (350°F).

02 Cut the crusts off your bread (or feel free to keep them on if you prefer). Press down the middle of each slice of bread with your fingers or the back of a spoon so it's flat; you should have a puffy border around the edge.

03 Dollop a teaspoon of chocolate hazelnut spread into the middle of each slice of bread and spread it out, avoiding the border.

04 In a small bowl, beat the egg and milk or water together to make your egg wash and brush it over the border with a pastry brush. This is essential to make the bread stick together.

05 Fold the bread in half and press the edges together with your fingers. You can also press the edges down with the back of a fork to seal them. They should look like little parcels.

06 Brush more egg wash over the top of the bread, then air fry for 5–6 minutes until crisp and golden brown.

07 Drizzle with melted chocolate hazelnut spread and dust with icing (powdered) sugar to decorate, if you wish. Serve with fresh raspberries, if using.

This recipe makes 3, but feel free to increase or decrease the quantity of ingredients to make as many or as few as you like.

SNACKING and SIDES

Recipes

Barbecue Chicken Wings	60
Loaded Potato Skins	62
Barbecue Chicken Nachos	64
Pizza Pockets	67
Sweet Potato Fries	68
Cheesy Stuffed Garlic Bread Sticks	70
Prawn Toast	72
Buffalo Cauliflower	75
Loaded Baked Potato	76
Coconut Shrimp	78
Pizza Bagel Bites	80
Loaded Cubed Potatoes	83
Cheese Twists	84
Mini Scones	86
Blooming Apples	88
Air Fryer S'mores	91
Flapjack Bites	92
Cinnamon Apple Chips	94

SO DELICIOUS!

Side dishes with main character flavour. From Cheesy Stuffed Garlic Bread Sticks and Loaded Potato Skins, to Cinnamon Apple Chips and Flapjack Bites, this chapter is full of sweet and savoury recipes that are perfect to bring to parties and events, or snack on in front of the TV.

Yum!

So saucy

BARBECUE CHICKEN WINGS

Serves 2

These are such a crowd-pleaser. Juicy, flavourful and perfectly messy. The whole fun of saucy wings is licking your fingers afterwards, right? They're perfect for game days, parties or just a date for one!

25 minutes + 2 hours marinating

450g (15oz) chicken wings
1 tsp olive oil
1 tsp sweet smoky paprika
1 tsp barbecue seasoning
2–3 tbsp barbecue sauce
Salt and pepper

TO SERVE:
Fresh chives, finely chopped
Sour cream (optional)

01 Put the chicken wings into a large bowl and coat in the oil, paprika, barbecue seasoning and some salt and pepper. Cover the bowl with cling film (plastic wrap) and pop it in the refrigerator for a couple of hours to marinate.

02 Remove the chicken wings from the refrigerator and preheat the air fryer to 180°C (350°F).

03 Place the chicken wings directly in your air fryer. Air fry for 20 minutes, carefully turning them over halfway through. They should be crispy and cooked through to at least 75°C (167°F) when tested with a meat thermometer.

04 In a bowl, toss the chicken wings in the barbecue sauce, then transfer to a serving plate.

TO SERVE:
05 Sprinkle with chopped chives and serve with sour cream for dipping, if you like. Enjoy!

LOADED POTATO SKINS

Serves 2

These potato skins take me back to my school days. I would stand in the middle of the cafeteria with the potato in one hand, spoon in the other, feeling quite content with my crispy, cheesy, bacon-y potato. Have these as a snack or a side dish, totally up to you – they're delicious however you eat them.

55 minutes

- 2 small or medium floury or baking potatoes (I use Maris Piper)
- Olive oil
- 15g (0.75oz) salted butter, softened
- 50g (1.75oz) Cheddar and/or mozzarella, grated
- 1 rasher of bacon, diced into small pieces
- Salt and pepper

TO SERVE (OPTIONAL):
- Sour cream
- Fresh chives, finely chopped

01 Preheat the air fryer to 170°C (340°F).

02 Scrub your potatoes, rub with the oil and some salt, then place them in your air fryer and air fry for 20 minutes. Up the temperature to 200°C (400°F) and air fry for another 12–15 minutes; the potatoes should be crisp on the outside and soft in the middle.

03 Carefully remove them from the air fryer and cut them in half horizontally, then scoop out the flesh into a medium bowl and set the skins aside.

04 Mix the potato flesh with the butter, some salt and pepper and half the grated cheese, then scoop the mixture back into the potato skins.

05 Sprinkle the remaining cheese and the diced bacon on top, then place the potatoes back in the air fryer.

06 Air fry for 10 minutes, or until the bacon is crispy and the cheese has melted.

TO SERVE (OPTIONAL):

07 Mix the sour cream with the chopped chives for the perfect dip and enjoy!

For a veggie option, swap the bacon for caramelised onion jam, minced garlic or a dollop of ready-made pizza sauce.

BARBECUE CHICKEN NACHOS

Serves 2-4

In the air fryer is my favourite way to make nachos. You just pile everything in, cook and they're ready to eat with almost no mess. Perfect for movie nights, parties or a quick lunch or dinner.

15 minutes

- 150g (5.25oz) tortilla chips
- Handful of cooked shredded chicken
- 2–3 tbsp barbecue sauce + extra to serve
- 1 large tomato, diced, or fresh ready-made salsa + extra to serve
- ¼ red onion, diced
- Handful of grated Cheddar and/or mozzarella

TO SERVE (OPTIONAL):
Guacamole
Sour cream

01 Preheat the air fryer to 180°C (350°F).

02 Measure out a piece of thick baking paper so it has a 10cm (4in) overhang all the way around your air fryer basket. If your air fryer doesn't have a basket, you'll need to use an airfryer-safe dish. Crumple the baking paper, then place it in your basket or dish with the edges folded up.

03 Tip your tortilla chips onto the baking paper, spreading them out evenly, then top with the cooked chicken, barbecue sauce, diced tomato or salsa and diced onion and sprinkle the grated cheese on top.

04 Air fry for 8–10 minutes until the cheese has melted and the chicken is piping hot; it should have an internal temperature of 75°C (167°F) when tested with a meat thermometer.

TO SERVE (OPTIONAL):

05 Remove from the air fryer and transfer onto a serving plate, then top with more barbecue sauce and diced tomato or salsa, with dollops of guacamole and sour cream, if you wish. Serve straight away. Enjoy!

PIZZA POCKETS

Makes 3

These pizza pockets are such a fun and easy snack, like mini calzones. They're super easy to make with just bread, egg and your favourite fillings. Ideal for when you fancy a pizza, but different, y'know.

15 minutes

- 3 slices of soft bread
- 1½ tbsp ready-made pizza sauce
- 30–40g (1.5oz) mozzarella, grated
- 6 slices of pepperoni, cut into pieces (or I use 1 mini Peperami stick, sliced)
- 1 small egg + 1 tsp milk or water, for the egg wash

01 Preheat the air fryer to 180°C (350°F).

02 Cut the crusts off your bread (or feel free to keep them on if you prefer). Press down the middle of each slice of bread with your fingers or the back of a spoon so it's flat; you should have a puffy border around the edge.

03 Dollop half a tablespoon of pizza sauce into the middle of each slice of bread and spread it out, avoiding the border, then add a third of the mozzarella and the pepperoni to each slice.

04 In a small bowl, beat the egg and milk or water together to make your egg wash and brush it over the border with a pastry brush. This is essential to make the bread stick together.

05 Fold the bread in half and press the edges together with your fingers. You can also press them down with the back of a fork to seal them. They should look like little parcels.

06 Brush more egg wash over the top of the bread, then air fry for 6–7 minutes until crisp and golden brown.

This recipe makes 3, but feel free to increase or decrease the ingredients to make as many or as few as you like.

SWEET POTATO FRIES

Serves 2, as a side

Sweet potato fries are my husband's absolute favourite. He'll always upgrade his regular fries to sweet potato if we go to a restaurant. They're so easy to make at home (without paying for the upgrade) and they taste amazing fresh out of the air fryer.

20 minutes

1 large sweet potato
1 tsp olive oil
Seasonings of your choice (smoked paprika, Cajun seasoning, barbecue seasoning or mixed herbs all work well)
Your favourite dips, to serve

01 Preheat the air fryer to 180°C (350°F).

02 Peel the sweet potato (or leave the skin on, it's totally up to you), then slice it into 1cm (½in) sticks. You can slice them thinner or thicker if you prefer, you will just need to adjust the cooking time slightly.

03 Put the sweet potato sticks into a large bowl, drizzle over the oil and sprinkle over your chosen seasonings. Toss the fries well to coat them evenly.

04 Put them in your air fryer, try not to overlap them too much. You may need to cook them in batches, depending on the size of your air fryer.

05 Air fry for 10–15 minutes until lightly golden and soft. Give them a toss a couple of times throughout cooking to ensure they cook evenly.

06 Serve immediately with your favourite dips alongside. Enjoy!

If cooking in batches, return all the fries to the air fryer and cook for a further 2 minutes to warm them up.

CHEESY STUFFED GARLIC BREAD STICKS

Serves 1-2

These garlic bread sticks are super soft and delicious. They're stuffed with gooey mozzarella and salty garlic butter. They're the perfect side dish for sharing and so quick and easy to make.

15 minutes

1 garlic clove, minced
20g (0.75oz) salted butter, softened
1 tsp chopped fresh parsley
Pinch of salt
2 slices of thick sandwich bread
30–40g (1.5oz) mozzarella, grated

01 Preheat the air fryer to 180°C (350°F).

02 In a small bowl, mix together the minced garlic, butter, chopped parsley and salt until combined.

03 Spread the garlic butter over both slices of bread, then sprinkle two thirds of the mozzarella over 1 slice of the bread. Place the other slice of bread on top with the garlic butter facing up, pressing down gently, then sprinkle the remaining mozzarella on top.

04 Air fry for 8–10 minutes until the mozzarella has melted and the garlic bread sticks are golden on top and the edges and base are crispy.

05 Slice it into 4 strips and serve warm. Enjoy!

PRAWN TOAST

Serves 4

Prawn toast is one of my favourite starters. Crispy bread topped with a delicious prawn (shrimp) mixture, air fried to golden perfection. Quick, easy to make and perfect for any occasion.

20 minutes

- 150g (5.25oz) raw prawns (shrimp), peeled and de-veined
- 1 tsp light soy sauce
- 1 garlic clove, minced
- 1 tsp minced fresh ginger or ginger purée
- 4 slices of sandwich bread
- 2–3 tbsp sesame seeds
- 1 medium egg
- Sweet chilli sauce, to serve

01 Preheat the air fryer to 200°C (400°F).

02 Mush up your prawns (shrimp) using a fork in a bowl or process in a food processor, then add the soy sauce, garlic and ginger and mix until combined.

03 Spread the prawn mixture over each slice of bread, then pour the sesame seeds into a bowl and fully coat the prawn side of the bread. Cut each slice of bread into 4 triangles.

04 Whisk the egg in a bowl, then dunk the bread in the egg, dripping off any excess.

05 Place the bread triangles directly in your air fryer and air fry for 7–10 minutes until the prawns are cooked and the toast is crispy.

06 Serve straight away with sweet chilli sauce. Enjoy!

BUFFALO CAULIFLOWER

Serves 4

A veggie twist on the classic buffalo wing. These cauli wings are crispy and tangy and packed with flavour. They're super easy to make and perfect for game day or just as a tasty side.

30 minutes

1 head of cauliflower, broken into bite-size pieces
2 medium eggs, lightly beaten
50g (5 tbsp) plain (all-purpose) flour
2 tsp paprika
80g (scant 1 cup) panko breadcrumbs
Olive oil spray
Salt and pepper

TO SERVE:
100ml (scant ½ cup) Buffalo sauce
1 tbsp sesame seeds

01 Bring a large saucepan of water to the boil, add the cauliflower and cook for 4–5 minutes. Drain the cauliflower and set aside.

02 Preheat the air fryer to 180°C (350°F).

03 Put the beaten eggs into one bowl. Put the flour, paprika and some salt and pepper into a second bowl and mix them together. Put the panko breadcrumbs into a third bowl.

04 Coat the cauliflower pieces in the seasoned flour, then in the egg, then in the breadcrumbs.

05 Spray your air fryer rack or basket with oil, then place the cauliflower pieces directly in the air fryer and spray again with oil. You may need to cook them in 2 batches.

06 Air fry for 10–15 minutes, turning them over halfway through, until crisp and golden brown.

TO SERVE:

07 Pour the buffalo sauce into a medium microwave-safe bowl and warm it through in the microwave. Then coat your cooked cauliflower in the sauce, transfer it to a serving plate.

08 Sprinkle with sesame seeds and serve straight away. Enjoy!

LOADED BAKED POTATO

Serves 1

A baked potato is the ultimate comfort food, isn't it? A humble potato, fluffy on the inside and crispy on the outside, topped with your favourite fillings – let your potato go wild!

45 minutes

1 large baking potato
  (Maris Pipers are also great)
Olive oil
Salt

FILLING SUGGESTIONS:
- The classic beans and cheese
- Tuna mayonnaise with sweetcorn
- Pizza-style with marinara sauce and grated mozzarella
- Chicken Fajita (use the filling on page 112)
- Beef Bolognese (see page 146) and cheese
- Tropical Shrimp (use the filling on page 144)

01 Scrub your potato, then prick the skin with a fork and rub it all over with olive oil and salt.

02 Place the potato on a microwave-safe plate and microwave on a medium–high heat (around 750W) for 8–12 minutes, depending on the size of your potato.

03 Preheat the air fryer to 170°C (340°F).

04 Place the potato in the air fryer and air fry for 25–30 minutes until crispy on the outside and fluffy in the middle.

05 Cut it open and add your favourite filling. Enjoy!

COCONUT SHRIMP

Serves 2

This is one of my favourite things to eat. Crispy, golden prawns (shrimp) coated in a crunchy coconut breading, perfect for dipping in a sweet and tangy sauce. Easy to make and absolutely delicious.

20 minutes

60g (½ cup) plain (all-purpose) flour
1 tsp salt
½ tsp black pepper
70g (1 cup) unsweetened coconut flakes
50g (½ cup) panko breadcrumbs
1 large egg
200g (7oz) raw prawns (shrimp), peeled and de-veined
Olive oil spray
Chopped fresh parsley, to garnish
Sweet chilli sauce, for dipping

01 In a large bowl, mix together the flour, salt, black pepper, coconut flakes and panko breadcrumbs. In a small bowl, lightly beat the egg.

02 Pat the prawns (shrimp) dry, dip them in the egg mixture, then coat them in the seasoned flour mixture, pressing it on well.

03 Preheat the air fryer to 200°C (400°F).

04 Spray the air fryer rack or basket with oil. Place the prawns in the air fryer in a single layer and spray with oil again.

05 Air fry for 7–9 minutes, turning them over halfway through, until crisp and golden brown.

06 Carefully transfer them to a plate, sprinkle with chopped parsley and serve with a pot of sweet chilli sauce to dip. Enjoy!

PIZZA BAGEL BITES

Makes about 10 mini bagels (20 bagel bites)
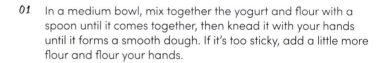

These pepperoni pizza bagel bites allow me to live my American dream. They're perfect for sharing, or not … They're quick and easy to make with just 2 ingredients for the dough and they're absolutely delicious.

20 minutes + 10 minutes cooling

- 80g (5 tbsp) Greek yogurt (I usually use Fage 0% fat)
- 80g (⅔ cup) self-raising flour + extra for dusting (optional)
- About 8 tbsp ready-made pizza sauce
- 40g (1.5oz) mozzarella, grated
- 6 slices of pepperoni, chopped into small pieces, or other toppings of your choice

TO SERVE (OPTIONAL):
Sour cream
Fresh chives, finely chopped

01 In a medium bowl, mix together the yogurt and flour with a spoon until it comes together, then knead it with your hands until it forms a smooth dough. If it's too sticky, add a little more flour and flour your hands.

02 Preheat the air fryer to 180°C (350°F).

03 Pick up about 2 tablespoons of the dough (or one tenth) and shape it into a flat disc, then push a hole through the middle. You want the bagels to be slightly thin and flat before baking, as they will rise and the holes will become smaller. Repeat to make the remaining mini bagels.

04 Place the mini bagels directly in your air fryer and air fry for 5–7 minutes until the tops are light brown and crisp and the bagels have risen.

05 Leave to cool for 5–10 minutes, as they will be very hot to touch, then gently slice them in half with a serrated knife.

06 Top each half with some pizza sauce, grated mozzarella and pepperoni or other toppings of your choice.

07 Air fry for a further 3–4 minutes until the mozzarella has melted. Leave to cool for a few minutes, then they're ready to eat.

TO SERVE (OPTIONAL):
08 Mix the sour cream with the chopped chives for the perfect dip and enjoy!

If you're adding light toppings that may fly around in your air fryer, place them under the cheese in step 6 to hold them down.

LOADED CUBED POTATOES

Serves 2

Crispy golden cubes of potato heaven, loaded with bacon, melted cheese, fresh chives and sour cream. Have as a side dish to share or a meal on its own, we don't judge here.

40 minutes

SPECIAL EQUIPMENT:
Air fryer-safe serving dish

- 2–3 medium floury potatoes (I use Maris Piper)
- 1 tbsp olive oil
- 1 tsp salt
- 50g (1.75oz) Cheddar and/or mozzarella, grated
- 1 rasher of bacon, diced into very small pieces
- Finely chopped fresh chives
- Sour cream or ranch dressing (optional)

01 Preheat the air fryer to 180°C (350°F).

02 Scrub your potatoes, then slice them into 2cm (¾in) cubes. Put them into a large bowl, then toss them in the oil and salt.

03 Transfer the cubed potatoes to your air fryer and air fry for 20 minutes.

04 Give them a shake, then turn up the heat to 200°C (400°F) and cook for a further 5 minutes.

05 Transfer them to the serving dish and spread them out evenly, then sprinkle with the grated cheese and chopped bacon.

06 Return to the air fryer and air fry for 6–8 minutes until the bacon is cooked through and the cheese has melted.

07 Sprinkle with chopped chives and add dollops of sour cream or ranch dressing, if you wish. Enjoy!

CHEESE TWISTS

Makes 8

Cheese straws are so nostalgic for me. They're something I enjoyed a lot as a kid. How can you not enjoy a crispy, cheesy, buttery stick of pastry? They're so easy to make and perfect for parties or an afternoon snack.

20 minutes

Olive oil spray
1 small egg + 1 tsp milk or water, for the egg wash
1 sheet ready-rolled puff pastry
20g Parmesan, grated
50g Cheddar, grated
2 tsp mixed herbs + extra to sprinkle (optional)
½ tsp salt

01 Preheat the air fryer to 180°C (350°F). Spray the rack or basket with oil.

02 Make your egg wash by beating together the egg and milk or water until combined.

03 Unravel the puff pastry, lay it out flat and brush the egg wash over the pastry.

04 Sprinkle the grated cheese, mixed herbs and salt over half the pastry in a thin layer, then fold it in half from the short edge and press it down gently.

05 Slice the pastry into 4cm (1½in) strips, then twist each strip a few times so it curls around itself. Place the twists in the air fryer.

06 Brush the twists with more egg wash then sprinkle with more mixed herbs if you wish.

07 Air fry for 10–13 minutes until crisp and golden, turning them over halfway through.

08 Best served fresh on the day, but you can store them in an airtight container at room temperature for up to 2 days. Enjoy!

MINI SCONES

Makes 5

Scones are genuinely one of my favourite foods. I used to make (and eat) them all the time with my great auntie. They're flaky and buttery, filled with your choice of raisins or chocolate chips. They're quick and easy to make and are guaranteed to brighten up your day.

25 minutes

SPECIAL EQUIPMENT:
5cm (2in) crinkle cookie cutter

115g (scant ¾ cup) self-raising flour + extra for dusting
30g (1.25oz) cold salted butter
1 tbsp caster (superfine) sugar
¼ tsp salt
75ml (¼ cup) milk + 1 tbsp, for brushing
50g (3½ tbsp) chocolate chips or raisins

TO SERVE (OPTIONAL):
Butter or clotted cream
Jam

01 In a large bowl, mix together the flour, butter, sugar and salt with your fingertips until it forms a crumbly breadcrumb texture. Stir in the milk with a spoon to form a soft dough, then fold through the chocolate chips or raisins.

02 Flour your surface, then gently knead the dough. Pat the dough down so it's about 2cm (¾in) thick, then use the cutter to cut out 5 circles. You may need to re-roll the dough to make 5.

03 Preheat the air fryer to 180°C (350°F).

04 Place the scones in the air fryer. You may need to cook them in 2 batches, depending on the size of your air fryer.

05 Brush the top of the scones with milk, then bake for 10–12 minutes until they're risen and golden brown on top. Leave to cool slightly.

TO SERVE (OPTIONAL):

06 Best served fresh, topped with butter or clotted cream and jam, if using. Enjoy!

07 Store in an airtight container for up to 3 days. You can also wrap them in cling film (plastic wrap) and freeze for up to 3 months.

BLOOMING APPLES

Makes 4

These blooming apples are such an easy and delicious dessert. They're sliced, baked with cinnamon and sugar, and open up like a flower. Top with your favourite ice cream and a drizzle of caramel sauce for the ultimate apple dessert.

30 minutes

30g (1.25oz) salted butter, melted
2 tsp light brown sugar
2 tsp granulated sugar
¼ tsp ground cinnamon
2 large apples of your choice

TO SERVE (OPTIONAL):
Ice cream
Caramel sauce

01 Preheat the air fryer to 180°C (350°F).

02 In a small bowl, mix together the melted butter, both sugars and the cinnamon until combined.

03 Slice each apple in half horizontally, then use a melon baller or a knife to remove the core without cutting through the whole apple.

04 Using a sharp knife, cut 2 circles around the inside of each apple about three quarters of the way down, it should look like you have 3 rings.

05 Turn the apples upside down on a chopping board, then slice down through the apples making cuts about 1.5cm (⅝in) apart.

06 Turn the apples upwards again and brush the cinnamon butter mixture generously over the top and place in your air fryer.

07 Air fry for 15–20 minutes. The apples should look soft and golden brown, and they should come apart (bloom) when pulled gently. Leave to cool slightly before serving.

TO SERVE (OPTIONAL):

08 Top with a ball of ice cream and drizzle of caramel sauce or serve however you wish. Enjoy!

AIR FRYER S'MORES

Makes 2

Gooey marshmallows, melted chocolate and crunchy biscuits. S'mores are so easy to make that this isn't really a recipe, but how could I not put something so delicious in this book?

10 minutes

- 4 digestive biscuits (or graham crackers)
- 2 extra-large (or 4 large) marshmallows
- 4–8 squares of chocolate of your choice (I like to use Lindt Excellent Extra Creamy Milk or Hershey's)

01 Preheat the air fryer to 160°C (325°F).

02 Place a sheet of thick baking paper in the air fryer. Place 2 of the biscuits next to each other on the paper.

03 Place the marshmallows on top of the biscuits, then air fry for 2–4 minutes until they're toasted to your liking.

04 Place the chocolate squares on top of the toasted marshmallows and let the heat from the marshmallows melt the chocolate. You could air fry for a further minute to help the chocolate melt if needed.

05 Remove them from the air fryer, place the remaining biscuits on top and serve straight away. Enjoy!

FLAPJACK BITES

Makes 8-10

These are so great to pop in lunch boxes or for a quick burst of energy when you need it. They're soft and chewy, packed with oats, honey or syrup and a mixture of your favourite fruit and nuts.

20 minutes

SPECIAL EQUIPMENT:
8–10 silicone or sturdy muffin cases

75g (2.5oz) salted butter
30g (2½ tbsp) light brown sugar
160ml (¾ cup) golden syrup or honey
140g (1¾ cups) rolled oats
50g (⅓ cup) mixture of dried fruit and nuts (e.g. dried cranberries, dried apricots, pecans, sunflower seeds)

01 Preheat the air fryer to 160°C (325°F).

02 In a medium–large saucepan, melt the butter, sugar and golden syrup or honey over a low–medium heat until the sugar has dissolved, and the mixture is smooth. Do not boil or overcook the mix.

03 Turn off the heat, then stir in the oats until they're fully coated, then stir through the mixed fruit and nuts.

04 Divide the mixture among 8–10 muffin cases and level them out. Air fry for 10–12 minutes until golden brown on top. Make sure you don't overbake them, otherwise tthe flapjack bites will be hard and crunchy.

05 Leave to cool to room temperature. Store in an airtight container at room temperature for up to 5 days.

Once cool, feel free to drizzle with your favourite melted chocolate.

CINNAMON APPLE CHIPS

Serves 1-2

Thinly sliced apples, dusted with cinnamon sugar, air fried to crispy perfection. They're super quick and easy to make in the air fryer and just irresistible.

20 minutes

1 large apple of your choice
1 tbsp granulated sugar
½ tsp ground cinnamon

01 Preheat the air fryer to 150°C (300°F).

02 Thinly slice the apple (about ¼cm/0.1in slices) and remove any pips.

03 In a small bowl, mix the sugar and cinnamon until combined.

04 Coat the apple slices in the bowl one by one, or sprinkle the cinnamon sugar over each side.

05 Place the slices directly in your air fryer, trying to space them out so they don't overlap too much.

06 Air fry for 12–15 minutes, turning every 5 minutes, until they're golden brown and starting to crisp up.

07 Leave to cool completely, as the apple chips will crisp up more as they cool.

08 Best served fresh, but they can be stored in an airtight container at room temperature for up to 5 days. Enjoy!

Feel free to double, triple or even quadruple the recipe to make more

SPEEDY LUNCHES

Recipes

Pizza Toastie	100
Hot Honey Chicken Tenders	102
Chicken Burrito	104
Crunch Wrap	107
Veggie Pastry Slices	108
Cajun-spiced Salmon Bites	110
Chicken Fajita Bakes	112
Naan Pizza	115
Ham & Cheese Toastie	116
Barbecue Chicken & Cheese Wrap	118
Brie, Bacon & Mango Chutney Panini	120

LEVEL UP YOUR LUNCH

~

Lunch just got quicker and easier with your air fryer. If you're bored of your current meals and fancy changing it up, this chapter is for you. From a Pizza Toastie to a homemade Crunch Wrap, and my favourite Brie, Bacon and Mango Chutney Panini (trust me, it's delicious), there's something to suit all tastebuds here.

Just perfect

Crunch!

PIZZA TOASTIE

Makes 1

This is one of my favourite lunches when I want pizza, but also a toastie ... Imagine melty cheese, zesty tomato sauce and your favourite toppings, all toasted between soft slices of bread. It's an easy and delicious meal and hits the spot every time.

15 minutes

- 2–3 tbsp ready-made pizza sauce
- 30–40g (1.5oz) cheese of your choice, grated (I use mozzarella and a little bit of Red Leicester)
- 8–10 slices of pepperoni or toppings of your choice
- ½ tsp dried oregano
- 2 slices of thick sandwich bread

01 Preheat the air fryer to 180°C (350°F).

02 Layer half the pizza sauce, grated cheese, pepperoni or other toppings and oregano on 1 slice of bread. Place the other slice of bread on top, pressing down gently.

03 Top with the remaining pizza sauce, cheese, pepperoni or other toppings and oregano.

04 Air fry for 10–12 minutes until the cheese has melted and the toastie is golden on top and the edges and base are crispy.

05 Cut in half and serve warm. Feel free to dip in your favourite sauce. Enjoy!

If using light toppings that may blow around in your air fryer, place them under the cheese in step 2 to hold them down.

HOT HONEY CHICKEN TENDERS

Makes 6-8

If you love a sweet and savoury combo like I do, these are for you. Crispy and juicy, coated in hot honey sauce, they're irresistible. Perfect for a quick dinner or snack, and you can make them as spicy (or not spicy) as you like.

25 minutes

1 large egg
60g (2½ cups) cornflakes
300g (10.5oz) chicken mini fillets
3 tsp paprika
1 tsp cayenne pepper
Salt and pepper

FOR THE SAUCE:
60ml (4 tbsp) honey
4 tsp dark soy sauce (light is also fine)
2 garlic cloves, finely minced
3 tsp hot sauce (more or less to suit your spice level)

01 Preheat the air fryer to 180°C (350°F).

02 Beat the egg well in a medium bowl.

03 Put the cornflakes into a food processor and process until roughly crushed. Alternatively, put them into a plastic bag and crush with a rolling pin. Pour into another medium bowl.

04 In a third medium bowl, coat the chicken fillets in the paprika, cayenne pepper and some salt and pepper, then coat them in the beaten egg, letting any excess drip off, then in the crushed cornflakes, making sure you pat really firmly on both sides of the chicken.

05 Transfer the coated chicken fillets to the air fryer rack or basket, making sure they're not touching each other, and air fry for 10–12 minutes until the chicken is cooked through to at least 75°C (167°F) when tested with a meat thermometer.

FOR THE SAUCE:

06 In a small-medium bowl, mix together the honey, soy sauce, garlic and hot sauce until combined. You can microwave it for about 20 seconds to warm it up and help it come together.

07 Coat the chicken tenders in the sauce.

08 Serve with your sides of choice. I love to use coleslaw. Enjoy!

CHICKEN BURRITO

Makes 1

Chicken, rice, veggies and sauce, all wrapped up in a warm, toasted tortilla. It's packed with flavour, quick and easy to make, and perfect for any time of the day – even breakfast, if you ask me!

25 minutes

- 100g (3.5oz) chicken, chopped into chunks (you can use pre-cooked)
- 100g (3.5oz) pre-cooked rice of your choice
- ¼ red onion, finely diced
- ¼ red (bell) pepper, deseeded and finely sliced
- 1 medium tomato, finely diced
- 1 tbsp mayonnaise or sour cream
- 1–2 tsp fajita seasoning or seasoning of your choice, such as Cajun or barbecue
- 1 large tortilla
- Olive oil spray

01 Preheat the air fryer to 180°C (350°F).

02 Place the chopped chicken in the air fryer and cook for 8–10 minutes until the chicken is cooked through to 75°C (167°F) when tested with a meat thermometer. If using pre-cooked chicken, skip this step.

03 Heat up your rice. I usually heat mine in the microwave.

04 In a small bowl, mix together the cooked chicken, warm rice, red onion, red (bell) pepper, diced tomato, mayonnaise or sour cream and seasoning until combined.

05 Lay your tortilla on a flat surface, then load the filling into the middle. Wrap it up: fold in the sides, then roll it up from the bottom, squishing the filling in as you roll.

06 Spray the air fryer with oil, then place the wrap, fold down, on the rack or in the basket and spray again.

07 Increase the temperature of the air fryer to 200°C (400°F) and cook for 5 minutes, or until crisp and golden.

08 Cut in half and enjoy!

CRUNCH WRAP

Makes 1

I do love myself a Taco Bell Crunchwrap, but why leave the house when you can make it at home? A toasted tortilla, packed with seasoned beef, cheese, lettuce, tomato and crunchy tortilla chips. It's easy to make and so delicious.

25 minutes

100g (3.5oz) minced (ground) beef
¼ onion, diced
1 tsp taco seasoning or similar
2 large tortillas
1 tbsp sour cream
A handful of grated Cheddar
4–6 tortilla chips
½ medium tomato, diced
A handful of shredded lettuce
Olive oil spray
Salt and pepper

01 Preheat the air fryer to 180°C (350°F).

02 Put the beef into the air fryer basket (or, if your air fryer doesn't have a basket, use a small air fryer-safe dish), then add the diced onion, some salt and pepper and the taco seasoning.

03 Air fry for 8–10 minutes until cooked through, stirring occasionally to break it up and help it cook evenly, then drain the excess liquid from the air fryer.

04 Lay 1 of the tortillas on a flat surface and cut a 10cm (4in) circle out of it to create a mini tortilla. Set aside.

05 Lay the remaining tortilla on a flat surface, dollop the sour cream into the middle, then spoon over the beef mixture. Sprinkle over the grated cheese, then place the tortilla chips on top in a circle no larger than your mini tortilla. Sprinkle the diced tomatoes and shredded lettuce on top, then finish with the mini tortilla.

06 Fold in the edges of the large tortilla, making creases as you work your way around the circle. It should look like a hexagon.

07 Spray the air fryer with oil, place the wrap, folds down, directly in the air fryer and spray with oil again.

08 Increase the temperature of the air fryer to 200°C (400°F) and air fry for 3–4 minutes, then flip it over and cook for another 2–3 minutes until crisp and golden on both sides; don't overcook them, otherwise the lettuce will wilt.

09 Cut in half with a serrated knife and serve. Enjoy!

Cut your leftover tortilla into triangles, spray with oil and air fry for 3–4 minutes, turning halfway through, to make your own tortilla chips.

VEGGIE PASTRY SLICES

Makes 6

Flaky pastry topped with colourful veggies and cheese, air fried to golden perfection. They're easy to make and perfect for any occasion, plus, what a way to add more veggies to your day.

30 minutes

1 sheet ready-rolled puff pastry
4 tsp ready-made green or red pesto
½ small red onion, finely sliced into rings
1 jarred roasted red (bell) pepper strip, finely sliced
1 mini courgette (zucchini), finely sliced
4 cherry tomatoes, sliced in half
1 x 100g (3.5oz) ball of fresh mozzarella
1 small egg + 1 tsp milk or water, for the egg wash
Olive oil spray
Fresh basil leaves, to garnish

01 Unravel your puff pastry, lay it out in a portrait position, then cut it into sixths (vertically down the middle, then horizontally into thirds to make 6 pieces). Feel free to refrigerate or freeze some of the squares for later if you don't want to cook them all straight away.

02 Score a 2cm (¾in) border around the edge of each piece of pastry and spread the pesto in the middle, then place the onion, red (bell) pepper, courgette (zucchini) and halved cherry tomatoes on top.

03 Break up the mozzarella and place little chunks on top of and around the veggies.

04 Preheat the air fryer to 180°C (350°F).

05 Whisk together the egg and milk or water for the egg wash, then brush it over the border.

06 Spray the air fryer with oil, then place the pastries on the rack or in the basket at least 4cm (1½in) apart and air fry for 15–18 minutes until they're puffed and golden brown. You may need to cook them in batches.

07 Garnish with fresh basil leaves and serve warm or cold. Enjoy!

CAJUN-SPICED SALMON BITES

Serves 2

I never thought I liked salmon that much, until I made these! Tender chunks of salmon seasoned with Cajun spices, paired with a creamy, sweet chilli mayo dipping sauce. Serve on a bed of rice and veggies ... or just eat them on their own, I won't judge.

15 minutes

FOR THE SALMON:
2 skinless salmon fillets (about 115g/4oz)
1 tbsp Cajun seasoning

FOR THE SAUCE:
1–2 tbsp mayonnaise
1 tsp sriracha
1 tbsp sweet chilli sauce

TO SERVE (OPTIONAL):
Cooked rice
Cooked edamame beans
Cucumber sticks
Chopped fresh chives

FOR THE SALMON:
01 Preheat the air fryer to 180°C (350°F).

02 Slice your salmon into 2.5cm (1in) cubes, then place them in a small–medium bowl and coat in the Cajun seasoning.

03 Feel free to line the air fryer rack or basket with foil or thick baking paper so the salmon doesn't stick. Place the salmon cubes in the air fryer and air fry for 7 minutes, or until cooked through to 45°C (113°F) when tested with a meat thermometer.

FOR THE SAUCE:
04 In a small bowl, mix together the mayonnaise, sriracha and sweet chilli sauce until combined.

TO SERVE (OPTIONAL):
05 I like to serve mine in a bowl, with rice, edamame beans, cucumber sticks and chopped chives, then drizzle the sauce over the top. You could also use the sauce as a dip. Enjoy!

CHICKEN FAJITA BAKES

Makes 4

All the flavours of chicken fajitas stuffed inside crisp and flaky puff pastry. These bakes are a great 'make ahead' meal or snack and they're absolutely delicious.

35 minutes

- 200g (7oz) chicken, chopped into chunks or small strips
- 1 red onion, finely sliced
- 1 red (bell) pepper, deseeded and finely sliced
- 1–2 tbsp fajita seasoning or seasoning of your choice, such as Cajun or barbecue
- 1 small egg + 1 tsp milk or water, for the egg wash
- 1 sheet ready-rolled puff pastry
- Olive oil spray
- Your favourite dips, to serve

01 Preheat the air fryer to 180°C (350°F).

02 Place the chopped chicken, red onion and red (bell) pepper in a medium bowl, then add the seasoning and coat everything well.

03 Transfer the mixture to your air fryer and cook for 8–10 minutes until the chicken is cooked through to 75°C (167°F) when tested with a meat thermometer.

04 Meanwhile, whisk together the egg and milk or water to make your egg wash and set aside.

05 Unravel the puff pastry, lay it out in a portrait position, then cut it into eighths (vertically down the middle, then horizontally into fourths to make 8 rectangles).

06 Divide the filling into the middle of 4 of the rectangles, leaving at least a 2cm (¾in) border around the edge.

07 Brush the border with some of the egg wash, then place the remaining 4 pieces of pastry on top, seal the edges with the back of a fork and prick the tops. Brush the tops with the remaining egg wash.

08 Spray the air fryer rack or basket with oil, then place the pastries in the air fryer at least 4cm (1½in) apart and air fry for 10–12 minutes until they're puffed and golden brown.

09 Serve with your favourite dips, such as sour cream, salsa or guacamole. Enjoy!

NAAN PIZZA

Makes 1

This is one of my favourite ultra-speedy lunches. Naan makes the perfect thick-crust pizza base, sturdy enough to hold all your favourite pizza toppings – even pineapple if that's your thing.

15 minutes

1 naan of your choice
2–3 tbsp ready-made pizza sauce
20–30g (0.75–1.5oz) mozzarella, grated
1 tbsp grated Parmesan
Sprinkle of dried Italian herbs

TOPPINGS (OPTIONAL):
Toppings of your choice, such as pepperoni, cooked chicken, red onion, diced (bell) pepper, ham, pineapple, mushrooms, fresh tomatoes

01 Preheat the air fryer to 180°C (350°F).

02 Place your naan in your air fryer, then top with the pizza sauce, grated mozzarella and toppings of your choice.

03 Air fry for 7–8 minutes until the cheese has melted and the base and edges are nice and crisp.

04 Carefully remove it from the air fryer, transfer to a plate, cut into quarters and sprinkle with the Parmesan and dried Italian herbs. Enjoy!

HAM and CHEESE TOASTIE

Makes 1

Ham and cheese toasties are so comforting. Warm, melty cheese and savoury ham, toasted to perfection between crispy slices of bread. Perfect for a quick lunch or dinner, this toastie never disappoints.

15 minutes

- 2–3 tbsp ready-made tomato and mascarpone sauce or sauce of your choice
- 2–3 slices of wafer-thin ham
- 30–40g (1.5oz) mozzarella or cheese of your choice, grated
- 2 slices of thick sandwich bread
- Your favourite sauce, to serve (optional)

01 Preheat the air fryer to 180°C (350°F).

02 Layer half the tomato and mascarpone sauce, the ham and half the grated cheese on 1 slice of bread. Place the other slice of bread on top, pressing down gently.

03 Top with the remaining sauce, then add the remaining cheese.

04 Air fry for 10–12 minutes until the cheese has melted and the toastie is golden on top and the edges and base are crispy.

05 Cut in half and serve straight away with a pot of your favourite sauce to dip, if using. Enjoy!

BARBECUE CHICKEN and CHEESE WRAP

Makes 1

Tender chicken, cooked with bacon and red onion, tossed in tangy barbecue sauce with melty cheese, wrapped in a soft toasted tortilla. I would happily eat this for my lunch every day.

25 minutes

SPECIAL EQUIPMENT:
Air fryer-safe dish

- 200g (7oz) chicken breast
- 1 tbsp barbecue seasoning
- Olive oil spray
- 1–2 rashers of bacon, chopped into small pieces
- 2 tbsp diced red onion
- 2 tbsp barbecue sauce + extra to serve (optional)
- Handful of grated mozzarella or cheese of your choice
- 1 large tortilla

01 Preheat the air fryer to 180°C (350°F).

02 Dice your chicken into 2.5cm (1in) cubes or slightly smaller, place them in a bowl and coat in the barbecue seasoning.

03 Spray the air fryer with oil, then place the chicken cubes, chopped bacon and diced onion inside. Air fry for 6–7 minutes until the chicken is cooked through to at least 75°C (167°F) when tested with a meat thermometer. Give the chicken, bacon and onion a shake or stir halfway through so everything cooks evenly.

04 Transfer the cooked chicken, bacon and onion to the dish, add the barbecue sauce and stir it through, then top with the cheese and place the dish into the air fryer.

05 Air fry for 3–4 minutes until the cheese has melted, stirring halfway through. Then give it another stir when it's done so it all comes together.

06 Spoon the mixture into the middle of the tortilla, then fold the wrap in from the sides and roll it up from the bottom, squeezing the filling in tightly, so you get nice tight wrap.

07 Place the wrap in the air fryer, with the fold facing down so it doesn't come apart, spray with oil and air fry for 3–4 minutes.

08 Cut in half with a serrated knife and it's ready to eat. Serve with extra barbecue sauce if you like. Enjoy!

BRIE, BACON and MANGO CHUTNEY PANINI

Makes 1

As a kid, I used to visit a café that served this combo and I fell in love with it. The flavours work so well together – the saltiness from the bacon, the creaminess from the Brie and the spiced fruitiness from the mango chutney ... it's perfection in panini form.

20 minutes

2 rashers of streaky bacon
1 panini roll or similar
2 tbsp mango chutney
5 slices Brie

01 Preheat the air fryer to 200°C (400°F).

02 Place the bacon in a single layer directly in your air fryer.

03 Air fry for 7–10 minutes, depending on how crispy you like your bacon. Carefully remove the bacon and set it aside on a piece of kitchen paper to drain.

04 Cut your panini roll in half and spread the mango chutney over both halves. Place your bacon on the base, top with the Brie, then place the other half of the roll on top.

05 Secure the panini with a toothpick at either end to hold it in place, then air fry for 5 minutes, or until the cheese has melted and it's cooked to your liking.

06 Carefully remove it from the air fryer, cut in half and enjoy!

Swap the mango chutney for cranberry sauce for a festive twist.

EASY DINNERS

Recipes

Peri-peri Chicken Burger	126
Mac 'n' Cheese	128
Veggie Noodle Stir-fry	130
Stuffed-crust Pizza	133
Tomato Gnocchi	134
Chicken Tender Tacos	136
Teriyaki Salmon	138
Toad in the Hole	141
Chicken Parm	142
Tropical Shrimp Tacos	144
Beef Bolognese	146
Hunter's Chicken	149
Stuffed Peppers	150

QUICK AND EASY

~

You guys know I'm all about keeping it simple when it comes to cooking, and I don't want to do extra washing up, so this chapter is full of quick and easy dinners that you will love, from Hunter's Chicken to a Veggie Noodle Stir-fry (which is one of my favourite savoury recipes in this book!).

So simple!

A classic

PERI-PERI CHICKEN BURGER

Makes 2

When you can't go to your favourite Portuguese chicken chain, make this burger at home! Juicy chicken in zesty peri-peri sauce, air fried to perfection, topped with halloumi, lettuce and tomato and served in a soft bun. Quick and easy to make and so delicious.

25 minutes

- 3–4 tbsp peri-peri sauce
- 4 slices of halloumi cheese
- 2 chicken breasts (about 150g/5.25oz each), flattened
- Olive oil spray
- 2 tbsp mayonnaise
- 2 ciabatta rolls or rolls of choice, halved
- 2 slices of a large tomato
- 4–6 lettuce leaves
- Your favourite sides, to serve

01 Preheat the air fryer to 200°C (400°F).

02 Put the peri-peri sauce into a bowl, then coat the halloumi in the sauce and set aside, then coat the flattened chicken breasts in the remaining sauce.

03 Spray the air fryer rack or basket with oil, then place the chicken in the air fryer, leaving room for the halloumi, and cook for 10 minutes.

04 Add the halloumi to the air fryer and cook both the chicken and halloumi for a further 5 minutes.

05 While they're cooking, spread mayonnaise over both halves of the rolls. When the chicken and halloumi are ready, place them on the bottom half of each roll, add a slice of tomato and some lettuce and top with the other half of each roll.

06 Serve with your favourite sides alongside. Why not try peas, Tenderstem broccoli, corn on the cob, spicy rice or some peri-peri fries? Enjoy!

MAC 'N' CHEESE

Serves 4

Whether you're having a good day or a bad day, mac 'n' cheese in the answer. This mac 'n' cheese is super cheesy and so easy to make. PS: add barbecue sauce on top afterwards ... you won't regret it.

30 minutes

SPECIAL EQUIPMENT:
Air fryer-safe dish

- 160g (5.50oz) dried macaroni
- 300ml (1¼ cups) water
- 120ml (½ cup) double (or heavy) cream
- 100g (3.5oz) Cheddar and/or Red Leicester, grated (you can use pre-grated cheese, but the end result won't be as smooth and creamy)
- 50g (1.75oz) fresh mozzarella, torn into chunks
- ½ tsp salt
- ½ tsp black pepper
- 1 tsp garlic granules

01 Preheat the air fryer to 180°C (350°F). Place the dish inside your air fryer.

02 Put the macaroni, water, cream, 75g (2.5oz) of the grated cheese and all the mozzarella, salt, pepper and garlic into the dish.

03 Air fry for 10 minutes, then stir through the remaining grated cheese and cook for another 10 minutes.

04 Remove it from the air fryer, give it a stir, then leave to sit for about 10 minutes. It will look liquidy at first, but don't worry, it will thicken as it cools. Enjoy!

Drizzle some barbecue sauce on top or stir it through for extra deliciousness.

VEGGIE NOODLE STIR-FRY

Serves 2

Stir-fry is one of my favourite dishes. I would cook it every night if my husband would let me. It's so flavoursome, packed with veggies and so easy to make. Feel free to add a protein, like chicken, prawns (shrimp) or steak.

35 minutes

SPECIAL EQUIPMENT:
Air fryer-safe dish

1 red or orange (bell) pepper, sliced into thin strips
1 large carrot, peeled and sliced into thin strips
1 small red onion, finely sliced
150g (5.25oz) green beans
1 head of broccoli, broken into small florets
1 tbsp olive oil
250g (9oz) fresh egg noodles
Salt and pepper

FOR THE SAUCE:
45ml (3 tbsp) honey
1 tbsp sweet chilli sauce
45ml (3 tbsp) light soy sauce
60ml (4 tbsp) water

01 Preheat the air fryer to 180°C (350°F).

02 Put all the vegetables in a bowl, then coat well in the oil and some salt and pepper. Put them directly into your air fryer and cook for 15–17 minutes until they're all tender.

FOR THE SAUCE:

03 While the vegetables are cooking, put all the ingredients for the sauce into a small bowl and mix them together, then set aside.

04 When the veggies are ready, remove from the air fryer and transfer to the dish. Add the noodles and the sauce and mix everything together so it's evenly coated in the sauce.

05 Place in the air fryer and cook for a further 5–6 minutes until the noodles are warm.

06 Divide between 2 bowls and enjoy!

STUFFED-CRUST PIZZA

Makes 1

I do love a good pizza. The thought of making a stuffed-crust pizza at home just makes me so excited. You can add as many or as few toppings as you wish, just bung the pizza in the air fryer and it's ready. No waiting for the delivery guy to knock at your door.

30 minutes

- 95g (scant ½ cup) Greek yogurt (I use Fage 0% fat)
- 80g (⅔ cup) self-raising flour + extra for dusting
- 4 cheese strings or long chunks of mozzarella
- Olive oil spray
- 60ml (¼ cup) ready-made pizza sauce or passata
- A handful of grated mozzarella
- Pizza toppings of your choice
- Dried Italian herbs or oregano, for sprinkling (optional)

01 In a medium bowl, mix together the Greek yogurt and flour with a spoon until it comes together, then knead it with your hands until it forms a smooth dough. If it's too sticky, add a little more flour and flour your hands.

02 Flour your surface and a rolling pin and roll out the dough thinly to just less than 5mm (¼ in) thick and shape it into a circle. Place the cheese strings or chunks of mozzarella around the edge of the circle, then fold the dough inwards over the cheese and press it down so it doesn't come apart. You can use toothpicks to help it stay in place if needed.

03 Preheat the air fryer to 180°C (350°F).

04 Spray the air fryer with oil, then place your pizza dough in the air fryer and spray with oil again. Air fry for 6–8 minutes.

05 Remove from the air fryer and spread on the pizza sauce or passata, then top with the grated mozzarella and toppings of your choice.

06 Air fry for a further 10 minutes, or until the cheese has melted and the dough is cooked through. Transfer to a serving plate and sprinkle over Italian herbs or oregano, if you wish.

07 Serve warm and enjoy!

TOMATO GNOCCHI

Serves 4

This gnocchi dish is so easy, so delicious and so comforting. You know I'm all for saving time, so I like to use ready-made gnocchi in this dish, but feel free to make your own.

25 minutes

SPECIAL EQUIPMENT:
Air fryer-safe serving dish

Olive oil spray
500g (1lb) fresh gnocchi
1 red (bell) pepper, deseeded and finely chopped
400g (14oz) ready-made tomato pasta sauce or passata or canned chopped tomatoes
1 tsp dried basil
50–60g (1.75–2oz) fresh mozzarella, torn into chunks
Salt and pepper
Fresh basil leaves, to garnish (optional)

01 Preheat the air fryer to 200°C (400°F).

02 Spray your air fryer rack or basket with oil, then put the gnocchi and chopped red (bell) pepper into the air fryer in an even layer and spray with oil again.

03 Air fry for 8–10 minutes, turning everything over halfway through, until the gnocchi are lightly golden and the pepper is tender.

04 Transfer the gnocchi and pepper to the serving dish, then stir in the tomato sauce, passata or chopped tomatoes, some salt and pepper and the dried basil. Place chunks of the fresh mozzarella on top.

05 Return to the air fryer and cook for a further 6 minutes, or until everything is piping hot.

06 Carefully remove the dish from the air fryer and garnish with fresh basil, if using. Enjoy!

CHICKEN TENDER TACOS

Makes 6-8

Crispy cornflake-crusted chicken tenders, shredded lettuce, fresh tomato and tangy sauce. These tacos are so quick and easy to make for a fun and delicious dinner.

25 minutes

FOR THE CHICKEN:
1 medium egg, beaten
60g (2½ cups) cornflakes
3 tsp paprika
300g (10.5oz) chicken mini fillets
Salt and pepper

FOR THE SAUCE:
2 tbsp mayonnaise
2 tsp ketchup
1 tsp yellow mustard
½ tsp paprika
1 tsp Worcestershire sauce

TO ASSEMBLE:
6–8 soft taco tortillas
Handful of shredded lettuce
1 large tomato, diced

FOR THE CHICKEN:

01 Beat the egg well in a medium bowl.

02 Put the cornflakes into a food processor and process until roughly crushed. Alternatively, put them into a plastic bag and crush with a rolling pin. Pour into another medium bowl.

03 In a third medium bowl, mix the paprika with some salt and pepper. Coat the chicken in the paprika mix, then coat them in the egg, letting any excess drip off, then the crushed cornflakes, making sure you pat them really firmly on both sides of the chicken.

04 Preheat the air fryer to 180°C (350°F).

05 Transfer the coated chicken fillets to the air fryer rack or basket, making sure they're not touching each other, and air fry for 10–12 minutes until the chicken is cooked through to at least 75°C (167°F) when tested with a meat thermometer.

FOR THE SAUCE:

06 In a small bowl, mix together the mayonnaise, ketchup, mustard, paprika and Worcestershire sauce until combined.

TO ASSEMBLE:

07 Place the taco tortillas on a serving plate, add shredded lettuce down the middle of each, followed by the chicken tenders, top with the diced tomato, then drizzle with the sauce, and they're ready to eat. Enjoy!

TERIYAKI SALMON

Serves 2

Teriyaki is one of my favourite sauces, but it's not just great for chicken. This salmon is sweet, savoury and so delicious. It's easy to make and deliciously satisfying. Serve with rice and your favourite veggies or whatever you wish.

15 minutes
+ 15 minutes marinating

2 salmon fillets (about 115g/4oz)
90ml (6 tbsp) teriyaki sauce
Olive oil spray
2 tbsp finely chopped spring onion (scallion)
1 tbsp sesame seeds
Cooked rice to serve

01 Place your salmon fillets in a bowl, then drizzle the teriyaki sauce over the top. Cover the bowl in cling film (plastic wrap) and pop it in the refrigerator for at least 15 minutes.

02 Preheat the air fryer to 180°C (350°F).

03 Spray the air fryer rack or basket with oil, then place your salmon fillets in the air fryer and brush them with the teriyaki sauce left in the bowl.

04 Air fry for 8–11 minutes until they're cooked through. If your salmon is particularly thick, it will need longer.

05 Sprinkle with sesame seeds and spring onion (scallion). Serve on a bed of rice, and enjoy!

TOAD IN THE HOLE

Serves 2

Toad in the hole is such a hearty classic, yet easy dish. Your favourite sausages, in a bed of Yorkshire pudding, served with gravy and a mixture of vegetables, if you like. This dish is perfect for two on any night of the week.

30 minutes + 15 minutes resting

SPECIAL EQUIPMENT:
15cm x 15cm (6in x 6in) baking tin (or one of a similar size that fits inside your air fryer)

1 large egg
50ml (¼ cup) whole or semi-skimmed milk
35g (3½ tbsp) plain (all-purpose) flour
20g (2½ tbsp) cornflour (cornstarch)
Olive oil spray
4 pork sausages
Salt and pepper

TO SERVE (OPTIONAL):
Your favourite veggies
Gravy

01 In a large bowl, whisk together the egg, milk, flour and cornflour (cornstarch) until smooth, then whisk in some salt and pepper. Let the batter rest for 15 minutes.

02 After 3 minutes, preheat the air fryer to 200°C (400°F).

03 Place the tin inside your air fryer and spray with oil. Place the sausages in the tin and air fry for 6–9 minutes until they begin to colour slightly.

04 Open the air fryer and turn the sausages over, then quickly pour over the batter. Air fry again for 15 minutes, or until the Yorkshire pudding is crisp and golden brown. It may need a few extra minutes, depending on your air fryer.

TO SERVE (OPTIONAL):
05 Serve with your favourite veggies and gravy and enjoy!

CHICKEN PARM

Serves 2

This is one of my husband's favourite things to eat. Crispy coated chicken breast topped with tangy marinara sauce and lots of gooey mozzarella. It's quick and easy to make and can be served with any side, from veggies and potatoes, to salad or pasta.

35 minutes

- 30g (3½ tbsp) plain (all-purpose) flour
- 1 large egg
- 40g (scant ½ cup) panko breadcrumbs
- 30g (1.5oz) grated Parmesan
- 2 medium chicken breasts (about 150g/5.25oz each)
- 2–3 thin slices of mozzarella
- Salt and pepper
- Chopped fresh parsley, to garnish (optional)

FOR THE CHEAT'S MARINARA SAUCE:
- 100ml (scant ½ cup) ready-made pizza sauce or passata
- 1 tbsp tomato purée
- 1 tsp dried oregano + extra to serve
- 1 tsp garlic granules or powder
- ¼ tsp onion salt

01 In a medium bowl, mix together the flour with some salt and pepper until combined.

02 In another medium bowl, beat the egg well.

03 Pour the panko breadcrumbs and grated Parmesan into a third medium bowl and mix them together.

04 Place the chicken breasts in between 2 sheets of baking paper and use a meat hammer to flatten them out. One at a time, coat them in the flour mix, then in the egg, letting any excess drip off, then in the panko breadcrumbs, making sure you pat really firmly on both sides of the chicken.

05 Preheat the air fryer to 180°C (350°F).

06 Transfer the coated chicken to the air fryer and air fry for 15–17 minutes until the chicken is cooked through to at least 75°C (167°F) when tested with a meat thermometer.

FOR THE CHEAT'S MARINARA SAUCE:

07 In a small bowl, mix together the pizza sauce or passata, tomato purée, oregano, garlic and onion salt until combined.

08 Dollop a few tablespoons of the sauce over each cooked chicken breast and spread it out to the edges, then place the sliced mozzarella on top.

09 Air fry for 5–6 minutes until the mozzarella has melted.

10 Remove from the air fryer and sprinkle with a little dried oregano and chopped parsley, if you like. Enjoy!

If you wanna be lazy, use pizza sauce in place of the cheat's marinara sauce.

TROPICAL SHRIMP TACOS

Makes 4

These tacos are inspired by one of my favourite places in Key West, Florida. They're super fresh and tangy and perfect for summer. The tacos are topped with fresh mango, crunchy cabbage and the most amazing citrus mayo. Just close your eyes and pretend you're on a tropical island while eating them.

15 minutes + 15 minutes marinating

- 250–300g (9–10.5oz) raw prawns (shrimp), peeled and de-veined
- 4 soft taco tortillas
- 2 handfuls of finely sliced red cabbage
- ¼ large fresh mango, peeled and sliced
- ¼ small red onion, finely diced
- Chopped fresh coriander (cilantro), to garnish

FOR THE MARINADE:
- ½ fresh mango (about 150g/5.25oz), peeled and roughly chopped
- Thumbnail-size piece of fresh ginger, peeled and sliced
- 30ml (1½ tbsp) water
- 1 tbsp rapeseed (canola) oil
- 1 tbsp honey
- 1 tbsp lime juice
- ½ tsp salt

FOR THE SAUCE:
- 1 tbsp mayonnaise
- ⅛ tsp lime juice
- ⅛ tsp lemon juice
- ¼ tsp honey
- Sprinkle of paprika

FOR THE MARINADE:

01 Place all the ingredients for the marinade in a blender or food processor and blend until smooth.

02 Put the prawns (shrimp) into a medium–large bowl, then pour over the marinade and coat the prawns well. Cover with cling film (plastic wrap), then refrigerate for at least 15 minutes or overnight.

03 Preheat the air fryer to 180°C (350°F).

04 Place the prawns in your air fryer in a single layer and air fry for 6–7 minutes, turning them over halfway through, until cooked through.

05 While they're cooking, assemble your tacos. Place the tortillas on a flat surface, then place some of the sliced red cabbage, sliced mango and diced onion down the middle of each one.

FOR THE SAUCE:

06 Make the sauce by mixing all the ingredients together in a small bowl.

07 When the prawns are ready, divide them evenly between the 4 tacos, garnish with chopped coriander (cilantro), then drizzle the sauce over the top or serve on the side. Enjoy!

BEEF BOLOGNESE

Serves 4

Bolognese has always been a favourite of mine. It's such a quick and easy, yet comforting dish. Rich, savoury beef in a thick tomato sauce, perfect over pasta with some Parmesan on top.

25 minutes

SPECIAL EQUIPMENT:
Air fryer-safe dish

500g (1lb) minced (ground) beef
½ onion, diced
1 clove garlic, minced
2 tbsp tomato purée
500g (1lb) passata or canned chopped tomatoes
1 tsp dried basil
½ tsp dried oregano
Salt and pepper

TO SERVE:
Cooked spaghetti or pasta of your choice
Grated Parmesan

01 Preheat the air fryer to 180°C (350°F).

02 Put your beef into the air fryer basket (or, if your air fryer doesn't have a basket, use a small air fryer-safe dish), then add the diced onion, garlic and some salt and pepper.

03 Air fry for 8–10 minutes until cooked through, stirring occasionally to break it up and help it cook evenly, then drain any excess liquid from the air fryer and transfer the beef mix to the dish.

04 Add the tomato purée, passata or canned tomatoes, dried basil and dried oregano and stir it through.

05 Air fry for a further 6–7 minutes until it's hot throughout.

TO SERVE:

06 Serve with cooked spaghetti or pasta of your choice and a sprinkle of grated Parmesan on top. Enjoy!

07 Store any leftovers in an airtight container in the refrigerator for up to 3 days.

HUNTER'S CHICKEN

Serves 2

Juicy chicken breast, stuffed with mozzarella, wrapped in streaky bacon, glazed with barbecue sauce. This is one of my favourite chicken dishes in this book, perfect for any night of the week.

30 minutes

- 2 medium chicken breasts (about 150g/5.25oz each)
- Olive oil spray
- 2 tsp barbecue seasoning or 1 tsp smoked paprika, ½ tsp onion powder and ½ tsp salt
- A small handful grated mozzarella
- 4 rashers of streaky bacon
- 2 tbsp barbecue sauce

01 Preheat the air fryer to 180°C (350°F).

02 Slice your chicken breasts three quarters of the way through to make a large pocket in each, then spray them with a little oil and coat the chicken breasts in the barbecue seasoning or paprika, onion powder and salt mix.

03 Stuff the pockets with the mozzarella, then close the pockets and wrap each chicken breast with 2 rashers of bacon.

04 Air fry for 18–20 minutes until the chicken is cooked through to at least 75°C (167°F) when tested with a meat thermometer. Brush the chicken with the barbecue sauce and air fry for a further 2–3 minutes.

05 Serve with the sides of your choice. Why not try corn on and fries? Enjoy!

STUFFED PEPPERS

Makes 2

My mum used to make these a lot and I loved them. Like a little pepper boat filled with tomatoey beef and cheese. They're so comforting and delicious, I might go ring my mum and see if she wants to make them with me.

40 minutes

SPECIAL EQUIPMENT:
Air fryer-safe dish

- 2 (bell) peppers or red sweet pointed peppers
- 225g (8oz) minced (ground) beef
- ½ small onion, diced
- 200g (7oz) canned chopped tomatoes
- 100g (3.5oz) ready-made tomato pasta sauce or passata
- 1 tsp dried Italian herbs
- 1 tsp garlic granules
- 120g (4.5oz) Cheddar and/or Red Leicester, grated
- Salt and pepper
- Chopped fresh parsley, to garnish (optional)

01 Preheat the air fryer to 180°C (350°F).

02 Prepare the (bell) peppers by slicing the tops off and removing the veins and seeds.

03 Put your beef and diced onion into the air fryer basket (or, if your air fryer doesn't have a basket, use a small air fryer-safe dish). Air fry for 8–10 minutes until cooked through, stirring occasionally to break it up and help it cook evenly. Drain the excess liquid from the air fryer and transfer the beef to the dish.

04 Add the chopped tomatoes, tomato pasta sauce or passata, Italian herbs, garlic granules and some salt and pepper. Stir everything through.

05 Air fry for a further 5 minutes, or until it's hot throughout.

06 Scoop the mixture evenly into your peppers and air fry for 10 minutes, or until the peppers are tender. Top with the cheese and cook for a further 2–3 minutes until the cheese has melted.

07 Sprinkle with chopped fresh parsley, if using, and serve. Enjoy!

BROWNIES, BLONDIES and COOKIES

Recipes

Soft Choc Chip Cookies	156
Fudgy Brownies	158
White Chocolate Blondies	160
Stuffed Cookie Pots	163
Choc Chip Shortbread Cookie Sandwiches	164
Speculoos Magic Bars	166
Sprinkle Cookie Sandwiches	168
Skillet Cookie	171
Double Chocolate Shortbread Cookies	172
Caramel Oat Cookie Bars	174
Mini Triple Chocolate Cookies	176
Thick NYC Cookies	179

LET'S GET BAKING!

This chapter gets me all excited! I absolutely love making a quick dessert, then just chucking it in the air fryer and letting it work its magic. A lot of these recipes are 'small batch', meaning they make a smaller than usual bake, which is great if you just want a dessert for two or don't want a full tray of blondies or brownies.

Delicious!

Perfect

SOFT CHOC CHIP COOKIES

Makes 12

If you wanna make cookies, but you only wanna make a small portion of them, this is the recipe for you. These cookies are soft and chewy with crisp edges, they're so delicious and they're super quick and easy to make.

30 minutes + 1 hour chilling

- 55g (1.75oz) unsalted butter, melted and cooled
- 75g (generous ¼ cup) light brown sugar
- 55g (¼ cup) granulated sugar
- ½ large egg (lightly beaten, then halved)
- ½ tsp vanilla extract
- 90g (¾ cup) plain (all-purpose) flour
- ¼ tsp bicarbonate of soda (baking soda)
- ¼ tsp salt
- 100g (7 tbsp) milk, white or dark chocolate chips + extra for the top

01 Put the melted butter and both sugars into a large bowl and mix together with a balloon whisk until the mixture forms a smooth paste (this may take a few minutes).

02 Add the egg and vanilla extract and stir until completely combined. The mixture should stay on the whisk for a few seconds before falling back into the bowl.

03 Sift in the flour, bicarbonate of soda (baking soda) and salt, then gently fold in with a wooden spoon or rubber spatula until just a few streaks of flour remain. Fold in the chocolate chips until evenly distributed (there should be no streaks of flour remaining at this point). Cover the bowl with cling film (plastic wrap) and chill in the refrigerator for at least 1 hour.

04 Preheat the air fryer to 160°C (325°F).

05 Place a sheet of thick baking paper in the air fryer. You may want to secure the baking paper down or fold it in half so it doesn't blow into your cookies. Working in batches, scoop up about 1 heaped teaspoon of the dough and place it on the baking paper. Repeat to make about 6 cookies per batch, spacing them roughly 5cm (2in) apart. Sprinkle more chocolate chips on top.

06 Bake each batch of cookies in the air fryer for 6–8 minutes until the edges are crisp and golden brown. The cookies will look puffy when they come out of the air fryer but will flatten and crinkle as they cool. Leave to cool for about 15 minutes before eating. Enjoy!

07 Store in an airtight container for up to 4 days.

What to do with half the egg? See page 19.

FUDGY BROWNIES

Makes 6-9

Rich, chocolatey, super-fudgy brownies, just smaller. These brownies are so easy to make and are so delicious! Perfect if you're short on time or don't want to turn your oven on.

45 minutes

SPECIAL EQUIPMENT:
15cm x 15cm (6in x 6in) baking tin (or one of a similar size that fits inside your air fryer)

70g (2.5oz) unsalted butter, melted and cooled slightly
100g (½ cup) caster (superfine) sugar
1 medium egg
50g (1.75oz) dark chocolate, melted and cooled slightly
40g (4½ tbsp) plain (all-purpose) flour
15g (2 tbsp) cocoa powder
¼ tsp salt
80g (6 tbsp) chocolate chips

01 Line the tin with thick baking paper.

02 Put the melted butter and sugar into a large bowl and beat together with an electric hand mixer for 2–3 minutes until fully combined and no lumps remain.

03 Add the egg and continue to beat until thick and fluffy (this could take from a few minutes up to 15 minutes, depending on the temperature of the ingredients and your equipment).

04 Mix in the melted chocolate until just combined. Sift in the flour, cocoa powder and salt, then gently fold in with a wooden spoon or rubber spatula until just a few streaks of flour remain. Then fold in the chocolate chips until evenly distributed and no streaks of flour remain.

05 Preheat the air fryer to 170°C (340°F).

06 Scoop the batter into your prepared tin and level it out, then place it in the centre of the air fryer and air fry for 13–15 minutes until the edges are cracked and it no longer wobbles.

07 Leave to cool completely and refrigerate for a few hours for a super-fudgy texture. Then cut into 6 or more pieces and enjoy!

08 Store in an airtight container at room temperature or in the refrigerator for up to 5 days.

WHITE CHOCOLATE BLONDIES

Makes 9

Super-fudgy, sweet, white chocolate blondies baked in a little tin. They're just so delicious and cute, perfectly baked in the air fryer.

45 minutes + 10 minutes cooling

SPECIAL EQUIPMENT:
15cm x 15cm (6in x 6in) baking tin (or one of the same size that fits inside your air fryer)

- 110g (4oz) white chocolate, broken into pieces
- 55g (2oz) unsalted butter
- 1 large egg
- 35g (2 tbsp) granulated sugar
- 1 tsp vanilla extract
- 80g (⅔ cup) plain (all-purpose) flour
- ½ tsp salt
- 100g (7 tbsp) white chocolate chips and/or chunks of white chocolate

01 Line the tin with thick baking paper.

02 Put the chocolate and butter into a microwave-safe bowl and microwave on low in 30-second bursts, stirring at each interval, until smooth and runny. If you overheat the mixture it can become lumpy or burn. Leave to cool for 10 minutes while you continue with the next steps.

03 In a large bowl, beat the egg with an electric hand mixer until light and foamy (this can take 5–10 minutes), then beat in the sugar and vanilla extract until combined. Pour in the cooled white chocolate mixture and beat until everything is completely combined.

04 Sift in the flour and salt, then fold in with a wooden spoon or rubber spatula. Add the chocolate chips and/or chunks and fold in until evenly distributed.

05 Preheat the air fryer to 150°C (300°F).

06 Scoop the batter into your prepared tin and level it out, then place it in the centre of the air fryer and air fry for 15–20 minutes until the edges are lightly golden and the middle no longer wobbles.

07 Leave to cool completely and refrigerate for a few hours for a super-fudgy texture. Then cut into 9 pieces and enjoy!

08 Store in an airtight container at room temperature or in the refrigerator for up to 5 days.

STUFFED COOKIE POTS

Makes 2

A gooey chocolate chip cookie in a ramekin stuffed with warm chocolate spread. My mouth is watering as I'm writing this. I have to admit, sometimes a cookie eaten with a spoon is better than a regular cookie (but if you're going to page 156 next, pretend you didn't read that).

25 minutes

SPECIAL EQUIPMENT:
Two 6cm x 6cm (2½in x 2½in) air fryer-safe ramekins

50g (1.75oz) unsalted butter, softened
40g (3 tbsp) light brown sugar
20g (1 tbsp + 1 tsp) granulated sugar
1 egg yolk
½ tsp vanilla extract
70g (½ cup) plain (all-purpose) flour
¼ tsp bicarbonate of soda (baking soda)
¼ tsp salt
60g (4½ tbsp) chocolate chips + extra for the top
2 tbsp chocolate spread or spread of your choice

01 In a small bowl, beat the butter and both sugars with a spoon to form a paste.

02 Add the egg yolk and vanilla extract and mix until combined, then fold in the flour, bicarbonate of soda (baking soda) and salt until just combined, then fold in the chocolate chips.

03 Preheat the air fryer to 160°C (325°F).

04 Divide the dough in half and place three quarters of each half into each ramekin and make a little well in the middle. Dollop 1 tablespoon of the chocolate spread into the middle of each, then place the remaining cookie dough on top and smooth it out. Sprinkle more chocolate chips on top.

05 Place in the centre of the air fryer and bake for 10–15 minutes until the top is crisp and golden brown.

06 Leave to stand for 2 minutes, then grab a spoon and dig in.

07 Best served straight away, but you can reheat them in the air fryer for 2–3 minutes up to 1 day after baking.

CHOC CHIP SHORTBREAD COOKIE SANDWICHES

Makes 6

Super soft, buttery, melt-in-your-mouth chocolate chip shortbread cookies, stuffed with chocolate hazelnut spread. These are absolutely to die for and they're so quick and easy to make.

25 minutes + cooling

- 55g (1.75oz) salted butter, softened
- 25g (1½ tbsp) granulated sugar
- 80g (⅔ cup) plain (all-purpose) flour
- 40g (3 tbsp) chocolate chips
- 30g (1½ tbsp) chocolate hazelnut spread or spread of your choice

01 Preheat the air fryer to 150°C (300°F).

02 Put the butter, sugar and flour into a large bowl and rub together with your fingertips until the mixture is completely combined and crumbly. Add the chocolate chips and fold in with a wooden spoon or rubber spatula until evenly distributed.

03 Pick up about 1 heaped teaspoon of the mixture and roll it into a flat disc shape. Repeat this with the remaining dough. You should make about 12 discs.

04 Line the air fryer with thick baking paper and place as many cookies as you can inside, leaving a 2cm (¾in) gap between them (they shouldn't spread much when baking). You may need to cook them in a couple of batches, depending on the size of your air fryer.

05 Air fry for 6–7 minutes. Make sure you don't overbake them, otherwise they'll become too hard and crunchy.

06 Leave to cool completely, then pipe your spread into the middle of half the cookies. Place the remaining cookies on the top and press down gently until the spread reaches the edges. Enjoy!

SPECULOOS MAGIC BARS

Makes 9

A buttery speculoos biscuit base, topped with condensed milk, chocolate chips, more speculoos biscuits and melted speculoos spread (cookie butter). These magic bars create such an amazing flavour and texture combo and they're so quick and easy to make.

40 minutes + cooling

SPECIAL EQUIPMENT:
15cm x 15cm (6in x 6in) baking tin (or one of a similar size that fits inside your air fryer)

125g (4.5oz) speculoos biscuits (I use Biscoff) + 6 extra, broken into pieces
50g (1.75oz) salted butter, melted
200g (7oz) condensed milk
150g (⅔ cup) milk and white chocolate chips
30g (2 tbsp) speculoos spread (cookie butter) (I use Biscoff), melted

01 Line the tin with thick baking paper and preheat the air fryer to 160°C (325°F).

02 Put the 125g (4.5oz) of speculoos biscuits into a food processor and process until finely crushed. Alternatively, put them into a plastic bag and crush finely with a rolling pin.

03 Tip into a medium bowl, then pour in the melted butter and mix together with a spoon until fully combined.

04 Scoop the mixture into your prepared tin and press down firmly with the back of a spoon. Pour over the condensed milk, then sprinkle over the chocolate chips and broken speculoos biscuits and press down with the back of a fork.

05 Air fry for 20–25 minutes until the edges are crisp. Leave to cool completely in the tin.

06 Drizzle with the melted speculoos spread (cookie butter), then cut into 9 squares and enjoy!

07 Store in an airtight container in the refrigerator or at room temperature for up to 5 days.

SPRINKLE COOKIE SANDWICHES

Makes 8

These cookies make me happy just to look at them. They combine three of my favourite things: cookies, buttercream and sprinkles. They're perfect for any occasion, especially if you have a sweet tooth like I do, and they're really easy to make.

40 minutes + cooling and 1 hour chilling

- 110g (4oz) unsalted butter, melted and cooled
- 150g (¾ cup) light brown sugar
- 110g (generous ½ cup) granulated sugar
- 1 large egg
- 1 tsp vanilla extract
- 180g (1⅓ cups) plain (all-purpose) flour
- 1 tsp bicarbonate of soda (baking soda)
- ½ tsp salt
- 200g (scant 1 cup) white chocolate chips
- 30g (1.5oz) sprinkles

FOR THE BUTTERCREAM:

- 75g (2.5oz) unsalted butter, softened
- 150g (1¼ cups) icing (powdered) sugar, sifted
- ½ tsp vanilla extract
- 1 tbsp milk
- 20g (0.75oz) sprinkles + extra to decorate (optional)

01 Put the melted butter and both sugars into a large bowl and mix together with a balloon whisk until the mixture forms a smooth paste (this may take a few minutes).

02 Add the egg and vanilla extract and stir until completely combined. The mixture should stay on the whisk for a few seconds before falling back into the bowl.

03 Sift in the flour, bicarbonate of soda (baking soda) and salt, then gently fold in with a wooden spoon or rubber spatula until just a few streaks of flour remain. Fold in the chocolate chips and sprinkles until evenly distributed (there should be no streaks of flour remaining at this point). Cover the bowl with cling film (plastic wrap) and chill in the refrigerator for at least 1 hour.

04 Preheat the air fryer to 160°C (325°F).

05 Place a sheet of thick baking paper in the air fryer. Working in batches, scoop up about 2 teaspoons of the dough and place it on baking paper. Repeat to make about 4 cookies per batch (16 in total), spacing them roughly 5cm (2in) apart.

06 Bake each batch of cookies for 7–8 minutes until the edges are crisp and golden brown. The cookies will look puffy when they come out of the air fryer but will flatten and crinkle as they cool.

FOR THE BUTTERCREAM:

07 Once the cookies are completely cool, beat the butter with an electric hand mixer until creamy, then beat in the sifted icing (powdered) sugar and the vanilla extract until smooth. Add the milk, if needed, to loosen it, then fold in the sprinkles. The buttercream should be thick, but pipeable.

08 Transfer to a piping bag with a large star nozzle and pipe a large swirl on top of half the cookies. Place the remaining cookies on top to make sandwiches, then press extra sprinkles into the sides of the buttercream to decorate, if you wish.

09 Store in an airtight container for up to 4 days.

SKILLET COOKIE

Serves 2

This always reminds me of my birthday parties at the hut that serves pizza. It's warm, gooey cookie with melted chocolate chips, topped with ice cream and sauce if that's your thing (personally I'm an ice cream on the side kinda gal). It's so easy, so delicious and perfect for sharing.

30 minutes + 10 minutes standing

SPECIAL EQUIPMENT:
15cm (6in) cast iron dish

50g (1.75oz) unsalted butter, softened
40g (3 tbsp) light brown sugar
20g (1 tbsp + 1 tsp) granulated sugar
1 egg yolk
½ tsp vanilla extract
70g (½ cup) plain (all-purpose) flour
¼ tsp bicarbonate of soda (baking soda)
¼ tsp salt
60g (4½ tbsp) chocolate chips + extra for the top

TO SERVE (OPTIONAL):
Ice cream
Chocolate or caramel sauce, for drizzling

01 Preheat the air fryer to 150°C (300°F).

02 In a small bowl, beat the butter and both sugars with a spoon to form a paste.

03 Add the egg yolk and vanilla extract and mix until combined, then fold in the flour, bicarbonate of soda (baking soda) and salt until just combined. Don't overmix.

04 Fold in the chocolate chips, then scoop the batter into the cast iron dish and spread it out evenly. Sprinkle more chocolate chips on top.

05 Place in the centre of your air fryer and bake for 10–15 minutes until the top is crisp and golden brown, it should still be slightly gooey inside.

06 Leave to stand for 10 minutes, then carefully remove it from your air fryer using oven gloves, the skillet will still be very hot!

07 Top with ice cream and drizzle with sauce if you wish. Enjoy!

08 Best served straight away, but you can reheat it in the air fryer for 2–3 minutes up to 1 day after baking.

DOUBLE CHOCOLATE SHORTBREAD COOKIES

Makes 5-6

I love these cookies so much. The chocolate spread with the white chocolate topping and the buttery shortbread cookie base, everything just works so well together. They're so quick and easy to make and they look amazing too.

25 minutes + cooling

SPECIAL EQUIPMENT:
9cm (3.5in) round cookie cutter

FOR THE SHORTBREAD:
- 55g (2oz) salted butter, softened
- 30g (2 tbsp) granulated sugar
- 85g (generous ⅔ cup) plain (all-purpose) flour + extra for dusting

FOR THE TOPPING:
- 60g (3 tbsp) chocolate hazelnut spread (I use Nutella)
- 50g (1.75oz) white chocolate, melted

FOR THE SHORTBREAD:

01 Put the butter, sugar and flour into a large bowl and rub together with your fingertips until the mixture is completely combined and crumbly.

02 Flour your surface and your rolling pin, then roll out the dough so it's about 5mm (¼in) thick. If your dough gets too hot and sticky, flour your rolling pin again and sprinkle some flour over the top of the dough to stop it from breaking.

03 Preheat the air fryer to 150°C (300°F).

04 Use the cutter to cut as many cookies as possible. Re-roll the dough then cut out more if you can. I usually get 5–6 cookies.

05 Place a sheet of thick baking paper in the air fryer and place as many cookies as you can on top, leaving a 2cm (¾in) gap between them. You may need to cook them in a couple of batches, depending on the size of your air fryer.

06 Air fry for 7–9 minutes. Make sure you don't overbake them, otherwise they'll become too hard and crunchy. Remove them from the air fryer and leave to cool completely.

FOR THE TOPPING:

07 Once the cookies are completely cool, dollop half a tablespoon of chocolate hazelnut spread on each cookie and smooth it out, almost to the edge, then dollop 1–2 teaspoons of melted white chocolate on top and gently smooth it out almost to the edges of the chocolate hazelnut spread. Leave to set at room temperature or pop the cookies in the refrigerator for 30 minutes to set faster.

08 Store in an airtight container at room temperature for up to 3 days.

CARAMEL OAT COOKIE BARS

Makes 9

I absolutely love oaty cookies, especially when paired with cinnamon and caramel. These are like a cookie in tray bake form, they're quick and easy to make and so delicious. I guarantee you'll want to make them again and again.

40 minutes

SPECIAL EQUIPMENT:

15cm x 15cm (6in x 6in) baking tin (or one of a similar size that fits inside your air fryer)

165g (5.5oz) unsalted butter, softened
165g (generous ¾ cup) light brown sugar
1 tsp vanilla extract
½ tsp bicarbonate of soda (baking soda)
½ tsp salt
135g (1 cup) plain (all-purpose) flour
80g (1 cup) rolled oats
1 tsp ground cinnamon
150g (½ cup) ready-made thick salted caramel sauce, melted
200g (scant 1 cup) milk or dark chocolate chips
Flaky sea salt, to sprinkle

01 Line the tin with thick baking paper and preheat the air fryer to 160°C (325°F).

02 In large bowl, mix together the butter and light brown sugar with a spoon or rubber spatula to form a paste.

03 Add the vanilla extract, bicarbonate of soda (baking soda) and salt and fold in, then fold in the flour, oats and cinnamon until just combined.

04 Divide the mixture in half and press one half into the base of your prepared tin, then smooth it out with the back of a spoon. Pour over the melted salted caramel sauce and smooth it out to the edges, then sprinkle over the chocolate chips.

05 Split the remaining dough into balls of varying sizes and scatter them evenly over the top. You don't need to press them down, as they will spread in the air fryer.

06 Place in the centre of the air fryer and air fry for 20–25 minutes until the top is golden brown.

07 Sprinkle some flaky sea salt over the top, then leave to cool completely in the tin. Cut into 9 pieces and enjoy!

08 Store in an airtight container at room temperature for up to 4 days.

MINI TRIPLE CHOCOLATE COOKIES

Makes 40

These are for the chocolate lovers out there. These cookies are super chocolatey, packed with all three kinds of chocolate chips. They're super easy to make, and they bake perfectly in the air fryer.

1 hour
+ 1 hour chilling

- 55g (2oz) unsalted butter, melted and cooled
- 75g (generous ¼ cup) light brown sugar
- 55g (¼ cup) granulated sugar
- ½ large egg (see page 19)
- ½ tsp vanilla extract
- 80g (⅔ cup) plain (all-purpose) flour
- 10g (4 tsp) cocoa powder
- ½ tsp bicarbonate of soda (baking soda)
- ¼ tsp salt
- 100g (7 tbsp) milk, white and dark chocolate chips

01 Put the melted butter and both sugars into a large bowl and mix together with a balloon whisk until the mixture forms a smooth paste (this may take a few minutes).

02 Add the egg and vanilla extract and stir until completely combined. The mixture should stay on the whisk for a few seconds before falling back into the bowl.

03 Sift in the flour, cocoa powder, bicarbonate of soda (baking soda) and salt, then gently fold in with a wooden spoon or rubber spatula until just a few streaks of flour remain. Fold in the chocolate chips until evenly distributed (there should be no streaks of flour remaining at this point). Cover the bowl with cling film (plastic wrap) and chill in the refrigerator for at least 1 hour.

04 Preheat the air fryer to 160°C (325°F).

05 Place a sheet of thick baking paper in the air fryer. Working in batches, scoop up about ½–¾ teaspoon of the dough and place on the baking paper. Repeat to make about 6 cookies per batch, spacing them roughly 5cm (2 in) apart.

06 Bake each batch of cookies for 6–8 minutes until the edges are crisp. The cookies will look puffy when they come out of the air fryer, but will flatten and crinkle as they cool. Leave to cool for about 15 minutes before eating. Enjoy!

07 Store in an airtight container for up to 4 days.

Feel free to freeze half the dough to make a smaller batch and bake the rest another day.

THICK NYC COOKIES

Makes 5

Crisp on the outside, soft and gooey in the middle, these thick NYC cookies are so quick and easy to make and you don't even need to chill the dough or turn your oven on! Winner winner cookie dinner … (I tried).

20 minutes

60g (2oz) unsalted butter, softened
80g (scant ½ cup) light brown sugar
20g (1 tbsp + 1 tsp) granulated sugar
½ large egg (see page 19)
1 tsp vanilla extract
200g (1½ cups) plain (all-purpose) flour
½ tsp baking powder
½ tsp bicarbonate of soda (baking soda)
1 tsp salt
140g (⅔ cup) chocolate chips and/or chunks of chocolate

01 In a large bowl, beat together the butter and both sugars until fully combined, then beat in the egg and vanilla extract until creamy.

02 Add the flour, baking powder, bicarbonate of soda (baking soda) and salt and fold in using a wooden spoon or rubber spatula until there are just a few streaks of flour left. You could also use your hands if easier. Then fold in the chocolate chips and/or chunks until there are no streaks of flour left.

03 Preheat the air fryer to 160°C (325°F).

04 Scoop up about 100g (3.5oz) or one fifth of the dough, squeeze it together, then roll it into a ball. Repeat to make 5 balls.

05 Place a sheet of thick baking paper in the air fryer and weigh down or clip down the edges to be extra safe. Place the balls on the baking paper about 7.5cm (3in) apart and bake for 8–10 minutes until the edges are golden brown. Leave to cool for at least 10 minutes before moving them.

06 Best served on the day, but you can store them in an airtight container at room temperature for up to 1 day. You can also reheat them in the air fryer at 150°C (300°F) for 2–3 minutes.

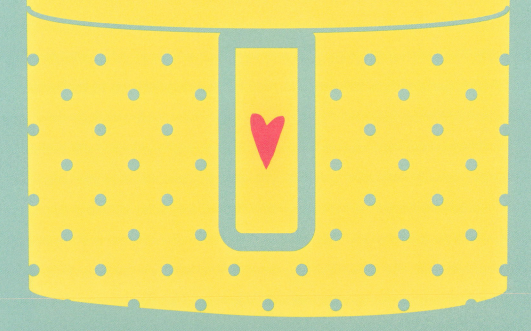

Recipes

Funfetti Cake	184
Chocolate Lava Cakes	187
Stuffed Banana Muffins	188
Mini Pastry Pies	191
Berry Crumble	192
Mini Cookies & Cream Cakes	194
Baked White Chocolate Mini Cheesecakes	196
Peanut Butter Lava Cakes	199
Mini Confetti Cakes	200
Puff Pastry 'Cronuts'	202
Speculoos Apple Crumble	204
Mini Speculoos Cakes	207
Banana Bread	208
Peach Cobbler	210
Chocolate Hazelnut Soufflés	212
Vanilla Cupcakes	215
Mini S'mores Pies	216

EASY AS PIE

~

Okay this might be my favourite chapter ... don't tell the other chapters though. It contains some of my favourite bakes, including Berry Crumble, Banana Bread, Stuffed Banana Muffins (there might be a theme going on here) and Peach Cobbler. They're all quick and easy to make and, of course, delicious!

So simple!

Mmmm...

FUNFETTI CAKE

Serves 8

A whole cake made in the air fryer! A great option for when you don't want to turn on your oven. Just make it like you would any other cake (only slightly smaller) and air fry away. Add your favourite toppings and you have the perfect cake for any occasion.

1 hour + cooling

SPECIAL EQUIPMENT:
3 x 15cm (6in) cake tins

FOR THE CAKE:
170g (5.75oz) margarine (I use Stork) or salted butter, softened
170g (generous ¾ cup) caster (superfine) sugar
170g (1⅓ cups) self-raising flour
½ tsp baking powder
3 large eggs
2 tsp vanilla extract
30g (1.5oz) sprinkles + extra to decorate

FOR THE BUTTERCREAM:
300g (10.5oz) salted butter, softened
600g (5 cups) icing (powdered) sugar
2 tsp vanilla extract

FOR THE CAKE:

01 Preheat the air fryer to 150°C (300°F).

02 In a large bowl, using an electric hand mixer, beat the margarine or butter and sugar until light and fluffy.

03 Beat in the flour, baking powder, eggs and vanilla extract until just combined. Try not to overmix, as this can knock the air out and create a dense cake, rather than a light and fluffy one. Fold through the sprinkles (see my tip about sprinkles on page 19).

04 Scoop the batter evenly into the cake tins and level it out.

05 Air fry the cake layers, one at a time, for 12 minutes, or until the top is lightly golden and a toothpick inserted into the middle comes out with a few moist crumbs. Set aside to cool while you cook the other layers. Leave them all to cool completely before making the buttercream icing. If your cakes have domes on top, you can level them with a knife or cake leveller.

FOR THE BUTTERCREAM:

06 Beat the butter with an electric hand mixer until creamy, then beat in the icing (powdered) sugar and vanilla extract until smooth. The buttercream should be thick, but pipeable. Transfer to a piping bag with a large star nozzle.

07 Transfer one layer of cake onto a cake stand or serving plate, then pipe a layer of buttercream over the top. Place the second layer of cake on top and repeat.

08 Place the third layer of cake on top, then decorate the top and sides of the cake with the rest of the buttercream. Top with extra sprinkles and enjoy!

09 Store in an airtight container at room temperature for up to 3 days.

CHOCOLATE LAVA CAKES

Makes 2

I love making stuff that looks fancy, but is actually really easy. You could serve these in a fancy restaurant and people would be impressed, I'm sure of it. But anyway, if you love chocolate, this is definitely for you.

30 minutes + 20 minutes cooling

SPECIAL EQUIPMENT:
Two 6cm x 6cm (2½in x 2½in) air fryer-safe ramekins

FOR THE RAMEKINS:
1 tsp unsalted butter, melted
2 tsp cocoa powder

FOR THE LAVA CAKES:
50g (1.75oz) semi-sweet or dark chocolate, chopped
50g (1.75oz) unsalted butter, cubed
1 medium egg + 1 medium egg yolk
50g (6½ tbsp) icing (powdered) sugar + extra for dusting (optional)
30g (3½ tbsp) plain (all-purpose) flour
10g (4 tsp) cocoa powder
Pinch of salt

FOR THE RAMEKINS:
01 Prep your ramekins by brushing them with the melted butter, then dusting them with cocoa powder, making sure it covers the inside of the ramekins, then tap out any excess.

FOR THE LAVA CAKES:
02 Preheat the air fryer to 170°C (340°F).

03 In a small bowl, melt the chocolate and butter (see page 19), stirring regularly until it comes together, then set aside to cool for 10 minutes.

04 In a medium bowl, beat together the egg, egg yolk and icing (powdered) sugar for a few minutes with an electric hand mixer until it thickens and turns light in colour.

05 Pour in the chocolate/butter mixture and stir until combined, then add the flour, cocoa powder and salt and stir until smooth. Scoop the batter into your 2 prepped ramekins, place them in the middle of your air fryer and bake for 10–13 minutes.

06 Carefully remove the ramekins from the air fryer (they will be very hot). The lava cakes should spring back when pressed gently. Leave to stand for 10 minutes.

07 Turn them out onto plates, dust with extra icing (powdered) sugar, if you wish, and serve straight away. Enjoy!

STUFFED BANANA MUFFINS

Makes 6

Banana muffins and cream cheese frosting just go hand in hand, you can't change my mind. These banana muffins are so soft and moist and cinnamony, filled with lots of sweet cream cheese frosting. Just the perfect combination and really easy to make.

**40 minutes
+ 10 minutes chilling (optional)**

SPECIAL EQUIPMENT:
6 large silicone or sturdy muffin cases

FOR THE MUFFINS:
- 110g (3.5oz) butter, melted and cooled
- 50g (¼ cup) granulated sugar
- 50g (¼ cup) light brown sugar
- 1 large egg, at room temperature
- 1 tsp vanilla extract
- 125g (1 cup) plain (all-purpose) flour
- 1 tsp ground cinnamon (optional)
- ½ tsp bicarbonate of soda (baking soda)
- ¼ tsp salt
- 2 medium ripe bananas, mashed
- 100g (7 tbsp) chocolate chips (optional)

FOR THE CREAM CHEESE FROSTING:
- 45g (1.5oz) unsalted butter, softened
- 45g (3 tbsp) full-fat cream cheese, at room temperature
- 125g (1 cup) icing (powdered) sugar, sifted

FOR THE MUFFINS

01 Put the melted butter and both sugars into a large bowl and mix together with a balloon whisk until combined, then mix in the egg and vanilla extract until just combined.

02 Sift in the flour, cinnamon, bicarbonate of soda (baking soda) and salt, then fold in with a wooden spoon or rubber spatula until only a few streaks of flour remain.

03 Fold in the mashed bananas until just combined. If adding any extras such as chocolate chips, fold them in here.

04 Preheat the air fryer to 150°C (300°F).

05 Scoop the batter evenly into the muffin cases and level out.

06 Air fry for 17–19 minutes until the tops are lightly golden and a toothpick inserted into the middle comes out with a few moist crumbs on.

07 Leave the muffins to cool slightly, then use the wide end of a piping nozzle to push down into the muffins and remove the inside (about two thirds of the way down).

FOR THE CREAM CHEESE FROSTING:

08 In a medium bowl, beat the butter and cream cheese with an electric hand mixer until creamy, then beat in the icing (powdered) sugar until smooth. Pop it in the refrigerator for 10 minutes, if you wish, to firm it up.

09 Transfer to a piping bag and snip off the end, then pipe it into the middle of each muffin.

10 Best served straight away, but you can store them in an airtight container for up to 3 days. Enjoy!

MINI PASTRY PIES

Makes 6

These may look a little like a popular breakfast tart that you pop in the toaster ... but, trust me, the homemade version is better. Yes, it might take a little longer to make your own, but it's worth it I promise, and we're already cheating by using ready-rolled pastry, so now we can get to the fun part faster ... eating it!

30 minutes + cooling

- 1 small egg + 1 tsp milk or water, for the egg wash
- 1 sheet ready-rolled shortcrust pastry
- 6 tbsp jam of your choice

FOR THE GLAZE:
- 130g (generous 1 cup) icing (powdered) sugar + extra, if necessary
- 2 tbsp warm water
- Pink food colouring (optional)

TO DECORATE:
- 2 tbsp freeze-dried strawberries or raspberries or sprinkles

01 Preheat the air fryer to 180°C (350°F).

02 To make the egg wash, lightly beat together the egg and milk or water until combined.

03 Unravel your pastry and lay out it out in a portrait position, then cut it into sixths (vertically down the middle, then horizontally into thirds).

04 Dollop a tablespoon of jam onto one side of each rectangle, fold them in half and seal the edges with the back of a fork, then prick the tops. Brush them with the egg wash.

05 Place a piece of thick baking paper inside the air fryer and transfer the pastries onto the paper at least 2.5cm (1in) apart (you may need to cook them in 2 batches).

06 Air fry for 15 minutes, or until they're cooked through. Carefully remove them from the air fryer to cool completely.

FOR THE GLAZE:
07 Make the glaze by mixing together the icing (powdered) sugar and warm water in a small bowl with a fork or spoon. The icing should be nice and thick. Add a dash of pink food colouring here, if using.

08 Dollop a blob of glaze onto each pastry and smooth it out gently, try not to let it run off too much. If your glaze is too runny, add more icing (powdered) sugar.

TO DECORATE:
09 Decorate with freeze-dried strawberries or raspberries or sprinkles. Leave the glaze to set and enjoy!

10 Best served fresh on the day, but you can store them in an airtight container at room temperature for up to 2 days.

Turn these into mince pies by swapping the jam for fruit mincemeat and the freeze-dried fruit for festive sprinkles.

BERRY CRUMBLE

Makes 2

Crumble is one of my favourite desserts. When I last went to California, there was one supermarket that made the most amazing berry crumble, and I must have eaten it at least five times. So that is what inspired this recipe and, trust, me it's absolutely delicious!

30 minutes

SPECIAL EQUIPMENT:
Two 6cm x 6cm (2½in x 2½in) air fryer-safe ramekins

FOR THE FILLING:
125g (4.5oz) fresh berries of your choice (I use blueberries, pitted cherries and raspberries)
30g (2 tbsp) granulated sugar
1 tsp cornflour (cornstarch)

FOR THE TOPPING:
40g (4½ tbsp) plain (all-purpose) flour
40g (3 tbsp) granulated sugar
35g (1.25oz) unsalted butter, cold and cubed

TO SERVE:
Cream or ice cream

01 Preheat the air fryer to 160°C (325°F).

FOR THE FILLING:
02 Mix together the berries, sugar and cornflour (cornstarch) in a small bowl until the berries are coated

FOR THE TOPPING:
03 In another small bowl, mix together the flour, sugar and cold butter until combined. I prefer to do this with my fingertips until it becomes crumbly.

04 Scoop the filling into the ramekins, then evenly crumble over the topping.

05 Air fry for 20–25 minutes until the tops are golden brown, then leave to stand for a few minutes, as they'll be very hot to touch.

TO SERVE:
06 Best served fresh and warm with your choice of cream or ice cream. Enjoy!

MINI COOKIES and CREAM CAKES

Makes 2

This is always a fan favourite on my Instagram. I mean how can you resist two soft little cakes made out of cookies and cream biscuits, topped with a sweet glaze? They're so quick and easy to make and perfect for any day of the week if you fancy doing a little bit of baking.

25 minutes

SPECIAL EQUIPMENT:
Two 6cm x 6cm (2½in x 2½in) air fryer-safe ramekins

FOR THE CAKES:
10 cookies and cream biscuits (I use Oreos) + extra biscuit crumbs, to decorate
½ tsp baking powder
100ml (scant ½ cup) milk (I use semi-skimmed)

FOR THE GLAZE:
50g (6½ tbsp) icing (powdered) sugar
1–2 tsp milk of choice or water

FOR THE CAKES:

01 Preheat the air fryer to 150°C (300°F).

02 Put the biscuits into a food processor and process until finely crushed. Alternatively, put into a plastic bag and crush with a rolling pin. Tip into a small–medium bowl.

03 Add the baking powder and milk and mix everything together with a spoon until smooth.

04 Evenly pour the batter into the 2 ramekins, then air fry for 15–17 minutes until a toothpick comes out with a few moist crumbs.

FOR THE GLAZE:

05 Mix together the icing (powdered) sugar and milk or water until smooth. You want it to be nice and thick, otherwise it'll slide off your cakes.

06 You can keep the cakes in the ramekins or scoop them out onto plates. Dollop the glaze on top of the cakes and smooth it out, then sprinkle with a few extra biscuit crumbs. Best served fresh on the day. Enjoy!

BAKED WHITE CHOCOLATE MINI CHEESECAKES

Makes 6

If you know me, you know I love a cheesecake. Usually I go for a no-bake cheesecake (which you can find lots of in my third book, *Fitwaffle's No-Bake Baking*, cough cough ...), but my husband loves a baked cheesecake, so he was very pleased to find these in the book.

25 minutes + 1 hour chilling

SPECIAL EQUIPMENT:
6 silicone cupcake cases

FOR THE BASE:
100g (3.5oz) digestive biscuits (or graham crackers)
40g (1.5oz) salted butter, melted

FOR THE FILLING:
225g (8oz) full-fat cream cheese, at room temperature
40g (5 tbsp) icing (powdered) sugar
1 large egg, at room temperature
1 tsp vanilla extract
50g (1.75oz) white chocolate, melted and cooled slightly

TO DECORATE:
200ml (scant 1 cup) double (or heavy) cream
Melted white chocolate (optional)
White chocolate curls (optional)
Fresh berries (optional)

FOR THE BASE:

01 Put the biscuits into a food processor and process until finely crushed. Alternatively, put into a plastic bag and crush with a rolling pin. Tip into a small bowl and mix with the melted butter until combined. It should look like wet sand.

02 Scoop the mixture evenly into the cases and press down firmly with the back of a spoon.

FOR THE FILLING:

03 In another bowl, beat together the cream cheese and icing (powdered) sugar with an electric hand mixer until smooth and creamy, then whisk in the egg and vanilla extract until fully combined, followed by the melted white chocolate.

04 Preheat the air fryer to 160°C (325°F).

05 Divide the mixture evenly into the cases, they should be filled to the top.

06 Carefully place them in your air fryer and air fry for 10 minutes. Allow the cheesecakes to cool slightly in the air fryer, then transfer them to a plate and refrigerate for at least 1 hour.

TO DECORATE:

07 To decorate, whip the cream to stiff peaks using an electric hand mixer, transfer to a piping bag with a large star nozzle and pipe a large swirl of cream onto the top of each cheesecake.

08 Drizzle with melted white chocolate and decorate with white chocolate curls or fresh berries, if you like.

09 Store in an airtight container in the refrigerator for up to 3 days.

PEANUT BUTTER LAVA CAKES

Makes 2

A twist on the original lava cake – peanut butter lovers, this is for you. Think of it like a peanut butter cup, but in cake form, chocolatey on the outside and peanut buttery on the inside. Absolutely heavenly.

30 minutes + 20 minutes cooling

SPECIAL EQUIPMENT:
Two 6cm x 6cm (2½in x 2½in) air fryer-safe ramekins

FOR THE RAMEKINS:
1 tsp unsalted butter, melted
2 tsp cocoa powder

FOR THE LAVA CAKES:
50g (1.75oz) semi-sweet or dark chocolate, chopped
50g (1.75oz) unsalted butter, cubed
1 medium egg + 1 medium egg yolk
50g (6½ tbsp) icing (powdered) sugar + extra for dusting (optional)
30g (3½ tbsp) plain (all-purpose) flour
10g (4 tsp) cocoa powder
Pinch of salt
2 tbsp smooth and creamy peanut butter + extra, melted, for drizzling (optional)

FOR THE RAMEKINS:

01 Prep your ramekins by brushing them with the melted butter, then dusting them with cocoa powder, making sure it covers the inside of the ramekins, then tap out any excess.

FOR THE LAVA CAKES:

02 Preheat the air fryer to 170°C (340°F).

03 In a small bowl, melt the chocolate and butter (see page 19), stirring regularly until it comes together, then set aside to cool for 10 minutes.

04 In a medium bowl, whisk together the egg, egg yolk and icing (powdered) sugar for a few minutes with an electric hand mixer until it thickens and turns light in colour.

05 Pour in the chocolate/butter mixture and stir until combined, then add the flour, cocoa powder and salt and stir until smooth. Scoop the batter into your 2 prepped ramekins, then dollop a tablespoon of peanut butter into each and press it in slightly so it's covered.

06 Place the ramekins in the middle of your air fryer and bake for 10–13 minutes.

07 Carefully remove the ramekins from the air fryer (they will be very hot). The lava cakes should spring back when pressed gently. Leave to stand for 10 minutes.

08 Turn them out onto plates, dust with extra icing (powdered) sugar or drizzle with some melted peanut butter, if you wish, and serve straight away. Enjoy!

MINI CONFETTI CAKES

Makes 2

When you just fancy a small bite of cake rather than a big one, these are the perfect snack. They're soft, sweet and moist, packed with sprinkles and you can decorate however you wish. Top with buttercream, like I did, or a simple glaze or eat them plain, totally up to you.

30 minutes

SPECIAL EQUIPMENT:
Two 6cm x 6cm (2½in x 2½in) air fryer-safe ramekins

FOR THE CAKES:
40g (4½ tbsp) plain (all-purpose) flour
30g (2 tbsp) granulated sugar
¼ tsp baking powder
40ml (3 tbsp) warm water
25g (1oz) butter, melted and cooled
½ tsp vanilla extract
10g (0.5oz) sprinkles

FOR THE BUTTERCREAM:
20g (0.75oz) unsalted butter, softened
40g (5 tbsp) icing (powdered) sugar
¼ tsp vanilla extract
Sprinkles, to decorate

FOR THE CAKES:

01 Preheat the air fryer to 140°C (275°F).

02 Put all the ingredients for the cake, except the sprinkles, into a small bowl and beat together until smooth, then fold through the sprinkles (see my tip about sprinkles on page 19).

03 Scoop the cake batter into the 2 ramekins. Level out the tops.

04 Place in the centre of the air fryer and air fry for 14–15 minutes until a toothpick inserted into the middle comes out with just a few moist crumbs. Leave to cool slightly, as they will be very hot to touch.

05 You can serve them in the ramekins or turn them onto plates.

FOR THE BUTTERCREAM:

06 Beat the butter with an electric hand mixer or a spoon until creamy, then beat in the icing (powdered) sugar and the vanilla extract until smooth. The buttercream should be thick, but pipeable.

07 Transfer to a piping bag with a large star nozzle and pipe a swirl on top of each cake, then decorate with sprinkles.

08 Best served straight away, but you can store them in an airtight container for up to 3 days. Enjoy!

Feel free to add a dash of food colouring to the buttercream to turn it any colour you like.

PUFF PASTRY 'CRONUTS'

Makes 4-5

I feel like cronuts are so fancy and I love that for them, but we're making the unfancy version, with good ol' ready-rolled puff pastry, and I love that for us. They're buttery, crispy, flaky and coated in lots of cinnamon sugar. They just melt in your mouth and they're so easy to make.

25 minutes
+ 15 minutes freezing

SPECIAL EQUIPMENT:
7.5cm (3in) round cookie cutter

1 sheet ready-rolled puff pastry
1 medium egg, beaten
45g (3 tbsp) granulated sugar
2 tsp ground cinnamon
30g (1.25oz) butter

01 Unravel the puff pastry, lay it out in a portrait position and brush the beaten egg all over.

02 Mark it horizontally into thirds, then fold the outer thirds inwards so they overlap and you have one long piece with 3 layers. Freeze this for 15 minutes.

03 Preheat the air fryer to 200°C (400°F).

04 Remove the pastry from the freezer and use a round cutter to cut out 4–5 circles from the pastry, then use a smaller circle or knife to cut out the middles.

05 Place them in your air fryer, spacing them at least 3cm (1¼in) apart, and air fry for 12–15 minutes until puffed and crisp.

06 While they're baking, mix together the sugar and cinnamon in a wide bowl and melt the butter.

07 When the 'cronuts' are baked, dip them in the melted butter, then coat them in the cinnamon sugar and they're ready to eat. Best served fresh on the day. Enjoy!

SPECULOOS APPLE CRUMBLE

Makes 2

Speculoos spread (cookie butter) and apples are such an incredible combo. I will literally just dunk slices of apple in melted spread, but these mini crumbles are definitely a step up from that. They're easy to make any day of the week, perfect for cuddling up on the sofa with.

35 minutes

SPECIAL EQUIPMENT:
Two 6cm x 6cm (2½in x 2½in) air fryer-safe ramekins

FOR THE FILLING:
- 15g (1 tbsp) granulated sugar
- ¼ tsp ground cinnamon
- 1 large apple, peeled, cored and cubed
- 20g (1½ tbsp) speculoos spread (cookie butter) (I use Biscoff) + extra to drizzle (optional)

FOR THE TOPPING:
- 40g (4½ tbsp) plain (all-purpose) flour
- 40g (3 tbsp) granulated sugar
- 35g (1.25oz) salted or unsalted butter, cold and cubed

01 Preheat the air fryer to 160°C (325°F).

FOR THE FILLING:

02 Mix together the sugar and cinnamon in a small bowl until combined, then add the cubed apple and toss until coated in the mixture.

FOR THE TOPPING:

03 In another small bowl, mix together the flour, sugar and cold butter until combined. I prefer to do this with my fingertips until it becomes crumbly.

04 Scoop the filliing into the ramekins, dollop the speculoos spread (cookie butter) over the top, then evenly crumble over the topping.

05 Air fry for 20–25 minutes until the tops are golden brown and the apples are soft, then leave to stand for a few minutes, as they'll be very hot to touch.

06 Feel free to drizzle more speculoos spread (cookie butter) over the top to decorate. Serve fresh and warm. Enjoy!

MINI SPECULOOS CAKES

Makes 2

One thing I love about this recipe (other than the fact these little cakes are incredibly soft and moist, taste delicious and are really easy to make) is that it can so easily be made vegan, just switch to non-dairy milk and, voilà, you have a vegan cake.

25 minutes

SPECIAL EQUIPMENT:
Two 6cm x 6cm (2½in x 2½in) air fryer-safe ramekins

FOR THE CAKES:
90g (6 tbsp) speculoos spread (cookie butter) (I use Biscoff), at room temperature
90ml (6 tbsp) milk of your choice
45g (4½ tbsp) plain (all-purpose) flour
½ tsp baking powder

TO DECORATE (OPTIONAL):
20g (1½ tbsp) speculoos spread (cookie butter), melted
Sprinkle of crushed speculoos biscuits

FOR THE CAKES:

01 Preheat the air fryer to 140°C (275°F).

02 In a small-medium bowl, mix together all the ingredients for the cakes with a fork or spoon until smooth. Make sure you don't overmix.

03 Scoop the cake batter into the 2 ramekins and level them out.

04 Air fry in the centre of the air fryer for 15–17 minutes until a toothpick inserted into the middle comes out with just a few moist crumbs.

TO DECORATE (OPTIONAL):

05 You can keep them in the ramekins or scoop them out onto plates. Decorate with the melted speculoos spread (cookie butter) and crushed speculoos biscuits, if you wish. Best served fresh and slightly warm. Enjoy!

BANANA BREAD

Serves 6-8

Banana bread is one of my favourite things to eat, but it has to be moist, none of this dry, crumbly stuff. I love adding cinnamon and white chocolate chips to my banana bread and eating it slightly warm – OMG.

1 hour 10 minutes

SPECIAL EQUIPMENT:
19cm x 9cm (7½in x 3½ in) loaf tin

110ml (scant ½ cup) rapeseed oil or melted butter
50g (¼ cup) granulated sugar
50g (¼ cup) light brown sugar
1 large egg, at room temperature
1 tsp vanilla extract
125g (1 cup) plain (all-purpose) flour
1 tsp ground cinnamon
½ tsp bicarbonate of soda (baking soda)
¼ tsp salt
2 medium ripe bananas, mashed
100g (7 tbsp) chocolate chips (optional)

01 Line the loaf tin with thick baking paper or a loaf liner. Preheat the air fryer to 150°C (300°F).

02 To make the cake batter, put the oil or melted butter and both sugars into a large bowl and mix together with a balloon whisk until combined, then mix in the egg and vanilla extract until just combined.

03 Sift in the flour, cinnamon, bicarbonate of soda (baking soda) and salt, then fold in with a wooden spoon or rubber spatula until only a few streaks of flour remain.

04 Fold in the mashed bananas until just combined. If adding any extras such as chocolate chips, fold them in here.

05 Pour the batter into your prepared loaf tin and level it out. Place it in the centre of the air fryer and air fry for 40–50 minutes until a toothpick inserted into the middle comes out with a few moist crumbs. Leave to cool in the tin for at least 1 hour, then transfer to a cooling rack to cool completely.

06 Store in an airtight container for up to 4 days.

To glaze the loaf, mix 50g (6½ tbsp) icing (powdered) sugar with 1 tbsp of boiling water, and drizzle over the banana bread before serving.

PEACH COBBLER

Makes 2

Peaches are one of my favourite fruits in desserts, they're so sweet and juicy. These mini cobblers are comforting and so delicious. The perfect after-dinner dessert in the air fryer. You can easily halve the ingredients to make 1 or double to make 4.

30 minutes

SPECIAL EQUIPMENT:
Two 6cm x 6cm (2½in x 2½in) air fryer-safe ramekins

FOR THE FILLING:
2 ripe peaches, peeled and diced
30g (2 tbsp) granulated sugar
½ tsp cornflour (cornstarch)
½ tsp vanilla extract
¼ tsp ground cinnamon

FOR THE TOPPING:
40g (4½ tbsp) plain (all-purpose) flour
15g (1 tbsp) granulated sugar
15g (1 tbsp) light brown sugar
¼ tsp baking powder
Pinch of salt
35g (1.25oz) unsalted butter, cold
¼ tsp vanilla extract

TO SERVE (OPTIONAL):
Cream
Ready-made caramel sauce

FOR THE FILLING:

01 In a medium bowl, coat the peaches in the sugar, cornflour (cornstarch), vanilla extract and cinnamon.

02 Divide the filling evenly into 2 ramekins; they should be about three quarters full.

03 Preheat the air fryer to 160°C (325°F).

FOR THE TOPPING:

04 In a small-medium bowl, mix together the flour, both sugars, baking powder and salt until combined, then add the cold butter and vanilla extract and mix it with your fingers until crumbly.

05 Spoon the topping over the peaches, making sure they're all fully covered.

06 Air fry for 15–20 minutes until the topping is golden brown and the peaches are bubbling.

TO SERVE (OPTIONAL):

07 Let them cool for a few minutes then serve warm with a drizzle of cream or caramel sauce, if you wish. Enjoy!

CHOCOLATE HAZELNUT SOUFFLÉS

Makes 2

This is one of my favourite low-ingredient recipes, you literally need 2 ingredients and you can make a delicious, light and airy chocolate pudding with a nice crisp top. Just grab a spoon, top with some icing (powdered) sugar and dig in.

30 minutes

SPECIAL EQUIPMENT:
Two 6cm x 6cm (2½in x 2½in) air fryer-safe ramekins

2 large eggs
170g (generous ½ cup) chocolate hazelnut spread (I use Nutella)
Icing (powdered) sugar, for dusting (optional)

01 Preheat the air fryer to 140°C (275°F).

02 Crack the eggs into a medium bowl and separate the yolks, placing them into a large bowl.

03 Using an electric hand mixer, beat the egg whites to stiff peaks and set aside.

04 Add the chocolate hazelnut spread to the egg yolks and mix them together with the electric hand mixer until fully combined; don't worry if it looks grainy and lumpy.

05 Gently fold in the egg whites a third at a time (try to keep as much air in the mixture as possible) until the mixture is nice and smooth and runny.

06 Scoop the mixture into the 2 ramekins and air fry for 18–20 minutes. The soufflés should still be wobbly in the middle and the tops should be crisp.

07 Leave to cool slightly, then dust with icing (powdered) sugar, if you wish, and serve. Enjoy!

VANILLA CUPCAKES

Makes 6

The air fryer comes in so handy when you fancy cupcakes but don't want to make a big batch. Just make sure you use some sturdy cupcake cases that hold your batter in place – I would recommend a small muffin tray, individual pudding moulds or silicone cases so the cupcakes hold their shape when baking.

40 minutes + cooling

SPECIAL EQUIPMENT:
6 silicone or sturdy cupcake cases

FOR THE CAKES:
- 110g (3.5oz) margarine (I use Stork) or unsalted butter, softened
- 110g (½ cup) caster (superfine) sugar
- 110g (scant ¾ cup) self-raising flour
- 2 large eggs, at room temperature, lightly beaten
- ½ tsp baking powder
- ½ tsp vanilla extract
- 1 tbsp whole milk

FOR THE BUTTERCREAM:
- 75g (2.5oz) unsalted butter, softened
- 150g (1¼ cups) icing (powdered) sugar, sifted
- ½ tsp vanilla extract
- 1 tbsp milk of your choice

TO DECORATE (OPTIONAL):
- Sprinkles
- Fresh fruit

FOR THE CAKES:

01 Preheat the air fryer to 140°C (275°F).

02 In a large bowl, using an electric hand mixer, beat together the margarine or butter and sugar until light and fluffy.

03 Beat in the flour, eggs, baking powder, vanilla extract and milk until just combined. Try not to overmix, as this can knock the air out and create dense cakes, rather than light and fluffy ones.

04 Scoop the batter evenly into the muffin cases and level them out.

05 Air fry for 18–20 minutes until the tops are lightly golden and a toothpick inserted into the middle comes out with a few moist crumbs. Leave the cakes to cool.

FOR THE BUTTERCREAM:

06 Beat the butter with an electric hand mixer until creamy, then beat in the icing sugar and the vanilla extract until smooth. Add the milk if needed to loosen it. The buttercream should be thick, but pipeable. Transfer to a piping bag with a large star nozzle.

TO DECORATE (OPTIONAL):

07 Pipe a large swirl on top of the cakes and decorate however you wish. I like to use sprinkles and fresh fruit.

08 Best served straight away, but you can store them in an airtight container for up to 3 days. Enjoy!

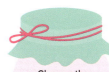

Change the flavour of your cupcakes by adding extras to the batter or the buttercream, such as lemon, fresh fruit or cocoa powder.

MINI S'MORES PIES

Makes 2

If you love biscuits, chocolate and marshmallows, you will love these little pots. They're so easy to make you barely need a recipe, but I couldn't not include them in this book.

15 minutes

SPECIAL EQUIPMENT:
Two 6cm x 6cm (2½in x 2½in) air fryer-safe ramekins

FOR THE BASE:
2 digestive biscuits (or graham crackers)
15g (0.75oz) salted butter, melted

FOR THE TOPPING:
75g (4 tbsp) chocolate hazelnut spread (I use Nutella) or similar
15g (¼ cup) mini marshmallows

01 Preheat the air fryer to 180°C (350°F).

FOR THE BASE:

02 Put the biscuits into a food processor and process until finely crushed. Alternatively, put into a plastic bag and crush with a rolling pin. Tip into a small bowl and mix with the melted butter. It should resemble wet sand.

03 Scoop the mixture evenly into the 2 ramekins and press down gently using the back of a spoon.

04 Air fry for 3–4 minutes. Be careful when you remove them, as they will be very hot.

FOR THE TOPPING:

05 Dollop 2 tablespoons of chocolate hazelnut spread on top of each base and spread it out to the edges, then sprinkle over a layer of mini marshmallows.

06 Air fry again for 2–3 minutes until the marshmallows are toasted to your liking.

07 Carefully remove them from the air fryer and leave to cool for at least 5 minutes before eating, as they will be very hot. Enjoy!

SEASONAL

Recipes

Chocolate & Strawberry Pastry Hearts	222
Easter Bunny Puff Pastries	224
Chocolate Egg Lava Pots	226
Mini Chocolate Egg Cookie Pots	229
Mummy Dogs	230
Halloween Boo-Biscuits	232
Pigs in Blankets with Honey Mustard Glaze	234
Yorkshire Puddings	237
Festive Sausage Rolls	238
Festive 'Leftovers' Toastie	240
Baked Camembert	242
Gingerbread Men	245
Not-Gingerbread Men	246

LET'S CELEBRATE!

~

It's party season! This chapter is full of sweet and savoury recipes that are perfect for celebrating, from Baked Camembert and Mummy Dogs, to Gingerbread Men and Easter Bunny Puff Pastries. This is such a fun chapter for every season.

Enjoy!

The G.O.A.T.

CHOCOLATE and STRAWBERRY PASTRY HEARTS

Makes 12

If someone made these for me for Valentine's Day, I would be smitten. You can't really beat flaky puff pastry, with fresh whipped cream, fresh strawberries and chocolate spread can you? These are really easy to make and really customisable too.

25 minutes + cooling

SPECIAL EQUIPMENT:
7.5cm (3in) heart-shape cookie cutter

1 small egg + 1 tsp milk or water, for the egg wash
1 sheet ready-rolled puff pastry
Granulated sugar, for sprinkling (optional)
250ml (1 cup) double (or heavy) cream, cold
30g (4 tbsp) icing (powdered) sugar + extra for dusting (optional)
12 tsp chocolate hazelnut spread (I use Nutella)
Strawberries, thinly sliced

01 Make your egg wash by beating the egg with the milk or water in a small bowl.

02 Unravel the puff pastry, then use the cookie cutter to cut out 12 hearts.

03 Preheat the air fryer to 180°C (350°F).

04 Transfer the pastry hearts into the air fryer, spacing them at about 3cm (1¼in) apart, and brush the tops with the egg wash. You can also sprinkle them with some granulated sugar, if you like. You will likely need to bake them in a couple of batches.

05 Air fry for 8 minutes, or until golden brown and puffed, then carefully remove them and leave to cool.

06 In a large bowl, whip the cream and icing (powdered) sugar to stiff peaks using an electric hand mixer and transfer it to a piping bag with a large star nozzle.

07 Carefully cut the cooled pastries in half using a serrated knife.

08 Dollop a teaspoon of chocolate hazelnut spread onto the base of each heart and smooth it out, then pipe on the whipped cream. I like to do 3 large blobs in a triangle. Place the sliced strawberries on top (3 per heart).

09 Place the pastry heart lids on top and dust with icing sugar if you wish. Then they're ready to eat. Best served fresh on the day. Enjoy!

Swap the chocolate hazelnut spread for speculoos spread (cookie butter) and the strawberries for raspberries for a different flavour combo.

EASTER BUNNY PUFF PASTRIES

Makes 10

I like to think of these as abstract Easter bunnies. As soon as you add the whipped cream bunny tail they start to come together, but until that point, you kinda have to use your imagination a little bit. They work so well with any spread and they're so fun for Easter time.

20 minutes

1 sheet ready-rolled puff pastry
50g (2½ tbsp) (or enough for a thin layer) chocolate hazelnut spread (I use Nutella)
1 small egg + 1 tsp milk or water, for the egg wash
100ml (scant ½ cup) double (or heavy) cream
20g (2½ tbsp) icing (powdered) sugar + extra for dusting

01 Unravel the puff pastry and thinly spread over the chocolate hazelnut spread, leaving a 1cm (½in) gap down the long edges.

02 Fold the pastry in half from the short edge and seal the edges with the back of a fork.

03 Use a knife or a pizza cutter to cut the pastry into 10 long ropes approximately 1.5cm (⅝in) wide.

04 Make a U shape with each piece, then twist the ends around each other. Think of the loop at the bottom being the bunny butt, the twist in the middle being its back, and the two ends at the top as the ears.

05 Preheat the air fryer to 180°C (350°F).

06 Make your egg wash by beating the egg with the milk or water in a small bowl, then brush it all over the pastries.

07 Place your pastries in the air fryer at least 3cm (1¼in) apart and air fry for 10–12 minutes until the pastry is crisp and golden brown. You will likely need to bake them in a few batches.

08 While they're baking, in a medium-large bowl, whip the cream and icing (powdered) sugar to stiff peaks using an electric hand mixer. Transfer to a piping bag with a large star nozzle.

09 Remove your pastries from the air fryer and leave to cool slightly, then pipe a large blob of the whipped cream onto the bunny 'butt' as a tail.

10 Dust them with extra icing sugar, if you wish, and they're ready to eat. Best served fresh on the day. Enjoy!

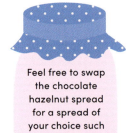

Feel free to swap the chocolate hazelnut spread for a spread of your choice such as speculoos spread (cookie butter) or peanut butter.

CHOCOLATE EGG LAVA POTS

Makes 2

I adore fondant-filled chocolate eggs, such as Creme Eggs. They're my favourite Easter chocolate, so why wouldn't I bake them into a soft, chocolatey cake? These lava pots are quick and easy to make and perfect for an Easter dessert.

30 minutes
+ 1 hour freezing
+ 20 minutes cooling

SPECIAL EQUIPMENT:
Two 6cm x 6cm (2½in x 2½in) air fryer-safe ramekins

2 fondant-filled chocolate eggs (I use Creme Eggs)

FOR THE RAMEKINS:
1 tsp unsalted butter, melted
2 tsp cocoa powder

FOR THE LAVA CAKES:
50g (1.75oz) semi-sweet or dark chocolate, chopped
50g (1.75oz) unsalted butter, cubed
1 medium egg + 1 medium egg yolk
50g (6½ tbsp) icing (powdered) sugar + extra for dusting (optional)
30g (3½ tbsp) plain (all-purpose) flour
10g (4 tsp) cocoa powder

01 Freeze the fondant-filled chocolate eggs for a least 1 hour.

FOR THE RAMEKINS:
02 Prep your ramekins by brushing them with the melted butter, then dusting them with cocoa powder, making sure it covers the inside of the ramekins, then tap out any excess.

FOR THE LAVA CAKES:
03 In a small bowl, melt the chocolate and butter (see page 19), stirring regularly until it comes together, then set it aside to cool for 10 minutes.

04 In a medium bowl, whisk together the egg, egg yolk and icing (powdered) sugar for a few minutes with an electric hand mixer until it thickens and turns light in colour.

05 Pour in the chocolate/butter mixture and stir until combined, then add the flour and cocoa powder and stir until smooth.

06 Preheat the air fryer to 180°C (350°F).

07 Scoop the batter into your 2 prepped ramekins, then gently press 1 frozen chocolate egg into each, on its side. Cover the egg with the mixture if you can still see it.

08 Air fry for 10–13 minutes, then carefully remove the ramekins from the air fryer (they will be very hot) and leave to stand for 10 minutes.

09 Turn them out onto plates, dust with icing sugar, if you wish, and serve straight away. Enjoy!

MINI CHOCOLATE EGG COOKIE POTS

Makes 2

Soft and gooey cookies, packed with chocolate chips and mini chocolate eggs. These cookie pots are so quick and easy to make and perfect just to bung in the air fryer. The ultimate Easter dessert.

25 minutes

SPECIAL EQUIPMENT:
Two 6cm x 6cm (2½in x 2½in) air fryer-safe ramekins

50g (1.75oz) unsalted butter, softened
40g (3 tbsp) light brown sugar
20g (1tbsp + 1 tsp) granulated sugar
1 egg yolk
½ tsp vanilla extract
70g (½ cup) plain (all-purpose) flour
¼ tsp bicarbonate of soda (baking soda)
¼ tsp salt
40g (3 tbsp) chocolate chips of your choice + extra for the top
40g (1.5oz) candy-coated mini chocolate eggs, crushed + extra for the top

01 Preheat the air fryer to 160°C (325°F).

02 In a small bowl, beat the butter and both sugars with a spoon to form a paste.

03 Add the egg yolk and vanilla extract and mix until combined, then fold in the flour, bicarbonate of soda (baking soda) and salt until just combined, then fold in the chocolate chips and crushed mini chocolate eggs.

04 Scoop the dough into the ramekins and sprinkle extra chocolate chips and crushed eggs on top.

05 Place in the centre of your air fryer and bake for 10–15 minutes until the top is crisp and golden brown. Leave to stand for 2 minutes (they will be very hot), then grab a spoon and dig in.

06 Best served straight away, but you can reheat them in the air fryer for 2–3 minutes up to 1 day after baking.

Seasonal

MUMMY DOGS

Makes 10

I absolutely love these. I just think they're so cute and perfect for Halloween. They're really easy to make, with just a few ingredients. Serve them at a Halloween-themed meal or party.

20 minutes

1 sheet ready-rolled puff pastry
10 hot dog sausages
1 small egg + 1 tsp milk or water, for the egg wash
20 edible eyes (optional)
Your favourite sauce, to serve

01 Unravel the puff pastry and lay out in a landscape position. Then cut vertically into 1.5cm (⅝in) strips using a knife or pizza cutter.

02 Place a sausage at the top of each strip, then wrap the pastry around the sausages, leaving a gap for the eyes and a few more gaps as you cross the pastry over.

03 Beat the egg and milk or water together to make the egg wash and brush it over the pastry.

04 Preheat the air fryer to 200°C (400°F).

05 Place mummy dogs in the air fryer in a single layer and air fry for 10–12 minutes until they're puffed and golden.

06 Carefully remove from the air fryer and add 2 edible eyes to each mummy dog, if you wish.

07 Serve with your favourite sauce and enjoy!

HALLOWEEN BOO-BISCUITS

Makes 14

These little ghosts are adorable, and they're so delicious! Soft, buttery, melt-in-your-mouth shortbread, topped with a sweet simple glaze. Perfect for making and decorating with the whole family.

25 minutes + cooling

SPECIAL EQUIPMENT:
7.5cm (3in) heart-shape cookie cutter

110g (3.5oz) salted butter, softened
60g (4 tbsp) granulated sugar
165g (1¼ cups) plain (all-purpose) flour + extra for dusting

FOR THE GLAZE:
130g (generous 1 cup) icing (powdered) sugar
2 tbsp warm water

TO DECORATE:
Black and red icing pens

01 Put the butter, sugar and flour into a large bowl and rub together with your fingertips until the mixture is completely combined and crumbly.

02 Flour your surface and your rolling pin, then roll out the dough so it's about 5mm (¼in) thick. If your dough gets too hot and sticky, flour your rolling pin again and sprinkle some flour over the top of the dough to stop it from breaking.

03 Preheat the air fryer to 150°C (300°F).

04 Use the cookie cutter to cut out 7 hearts, then cut each heart straight down the middle with a knife and gently push the tail around to one side. You can push the dough into the exact shape you want for your ghosts.

05 Line the air fryer with thick baking paper and place as many biscuits as you can on top, leaving a 2cm (¾in) gap between them. You may need to cook them in a couple of batches, depending on the size of your air fryer.

06 Air fry for 6–8 minutes. Make sure you don't overbake them, otherwise they'll become too hard and crunchy. Remove them from the air fryer and leave to cool completely.

FOR THE GLAZE:

07 Meanwhile, make the glaze in a small bowl by mixing together the icing (powdered) sugar and warm water, adding the water gradually until you get the right consistency – it should be nice and thick so it doesn't run off the biscuits. Transfer to a piping bag with a small round nozzle. If you don't have a suitable nozzle you can snip a tiny hole in the end of the piping bag.

08 Once the biscuits are cool, pipe an outline of glaze on the biscuits. Don't go too close to the edges, otherwise it can run off, then fill in the middle. It's best to use a thin layer of glaze as this will set better and there's less chance of it spilling over.

TO DECORATE:

09 Use a black icing pen to draw 2 eyes and a mouth. You can also use a red icing pen to draw 2 dots for the cheeks. Let the glaze set and enjoy!

10 Store in an airtight container at room temperature for up to 3 days.

PIGS IN BLANKETS *with* HONEY MUSTARD GLAZE

Makes 6

These are one of my favourite things about Christmas dinner. I will happily let someone have the last roast potato if I can have the last pig in blanket. Yes, they are just sausages wrapped in bacon, but these are also brushed with a honey mustard glaze and I'm definitely not waiting until Christmas to make these again.

20 minutes

- 6 thin sausages (both skinless or skin on are fine)
- 6 rashers of streaky bacon
- 30ml (2 tbsp) honey
- 2 tsp yellow mustard
- Olive oil spray

01 If using skin-on sausages, prick them all over with a fork. Wrap each sausage in a rasher of bacon, starting from one end and wrapping it up the sausage until it's covered.

02 Preheat the air fryer to 180°C (350°F).

03 Mix together the honey and mustard in a small bowl, then brush half of the glaze over the pigs in blankets.

04 Spray the air fryer rack or basket with oil, then place the pigs in blankets directly in the air fryer in a single layer.

05 Air fry for 5–7 minutes, then turn them over and brush the other side with the remaining glaze. Cook for a further 5–7 minutes until cooked through and the internal temperature reaches 75°C (167°F) when tested with a meat thermometer. Serve straight away and enjoy!

YORKSHIRE PUDDINGS

Makes 6

On Christmas day or whenever you're making a roast dinner, your air fryer is your new sidekick. These Yorkshire puddings come out perfectly risen and crisp every time.

25 minutes + 15 minutes standing

SPECIAL EQUIPMENT:
6 individual metal pudding tins

95g (¾ cup) plain (all-purpose) flour
1 small egg
180ml (¾ cup) whole milk
1 tbsp beef dripping
Salt and pepper

01 Put the flour into a medium bowl and mix with some salt and pepper.

02 Make a well in the middle of the flour with the back of a spoon and crack the egg into the middle.

03 Using a fork or balloon whisk, mix the egg into the flour, starting from the middle and gradually incorporating all the flour until it's fully combined.

04 Slowly pour in the milk, continuing to mix as you pour, until the batter is smooth, runny and lump-free.

05 Leave to sit for about 15 minutes to help the puddings rise.

06 Preheat the air fryer to 200°C (400°F).

07 Divide the beef dripping into the pudding tins, then place in the air fryer. Air fry for 8 minutes until the fat is sizzling hot.

08 As soon as the fat is hot, quickly pour the batter evenly into each prepared tin and air fry for 10 minutes. Then carefully turn the puddings over with tongs to brown the bottoms and cook for a further 4–5 minutes until crisp and golden brown.

09 Serve with your favourite dish or eat them on their own … there's no judgement here. Enjoy!

FESTIVE SAUSAGE ROLLS

Makes 8

My great auntie would always make the best sausage rolls. Ready-rolled puff pastry and cheap, skinless sausages. I'm adding cranberry sauce to these as well, because I'm a cranberry sauce fiend. I even eat it in ham sandwiches, but you do you, it's totally optional.

35 minutes

- 1 small egg + 1 tsp milk or water, for the egg wash
- 1 sheet ready-rolled puff pastry
- 8 tbsp cranberry sauce
- 8 thin skinless sausages

01 To make the egg wash, lightly beat together the egg and milk or water until combined.

02 Unravel your pastry and lay it out in a portrait position, then slice it into eighths (vertically down the middle, then horizontally into thirds).

03 Dollop a tablespoon of cranberry sauce at the end of each piece and spread it out. Place a sausage on top and fold the pastry over the sausage. Seal the the edges with the back of a fork, then make 3–4 slits in the top of the pastry.

04 Preheat the air fryer to 180°C (350°F).

05 Brush the rolls with the egg wash. Place them in the air fryer at least 2.5–5cm (1–2in) apart.

06 Air fry for 20–25 minutes, or until they're cooked through.

07 Carefully remove them from the air fryer to cool. Serve warm or cold and enjoy!

08 Best served fresh on the day, but you can store them in an airtight container in the refrigerator for up to 2 days.

FESTIVE 'LEFTOVERS' TOASTIE

Makes 1

What's the best thing about Boxing Day? A festive leftovers sandwich, of course. You can heat stuff up in the air fryer and you can make the ultimate toasted sandwich. Just bung in whatever you have and toast it to perfection. Don't forget to dip it in gravy!

15 minutes

1 tbsp mayonnaise
1 tbsp cranberry sauce
2 slices of thick bread
2–3 thick slices of cooked turkey
3–4 tbsp cooked stuffing
2 rashers of cooked bacon or 2 Pigs in Blankets (see page 234)
Butter, softened, or spreadable butter, for spreading
Gravy, to dip (optional)

01 Preheat the air fryer to 180°C (350°F).

02 Spread the mayonnaise and cranberry sauce over both slices of bread, then layer the turkey, stuffing and bacon or pigs in blankets on top of 1 slice of bread. Place the other slice of bread on top to make a sandwich.

03 Spread a layer of butter over the top, then place directly in the air fryer and air fry for 10 minutes, or until the meat is hot throughout and the bread is crisp and golden on top.

04 Cut in half and serve with a pot of gravy to dip, if you like. Enjoy!

BAKED CAMEMBERT

Serves 2-4

This is one of my favourite sharing starters at any restaurant. I love it when they give you lots of different dipping foods too. It's so quick and easy to make in the air fryer, perfect for parties or a cosy night in.

15 minutes

- 1 wheel of Camembert
- 1 tsp olive oil
- 1 tbsp honey
- Salt and pepper
- 1 small ciabatta bread or baguette, to serve (optional)

01 Preheat the air fryer to 180°C (350°F).

02 Remove the Camembert from its wooden box, unwrap, then place it back in the bottom half of the box.

03 Slice across the top into eighths, then drizzle with the oil, honey and some salt and pepper.

04 If using, cut your bread into dippable slices, then air fry the Camembert and the bread for 10–12 minutes.

05 Dip the toasted bread in the Camembert and enjoy!

Add walnuts to the top of the Camembert or switch up the flavours with cranberry sauce instead of olive oil and honey.

GINGERBREAD MEN

Makes 6-10

Ah, the classic gingerbread men. It would be criminal for me not to tell you how easy it is to bake these little guys in the air fryer. We're making a small batch here, but feel free to double the recipe to make more for a larger crowd.

30 minutes + 3 hours chilling + cooling

SPECIAL EQUIPMENT:
10cm (4in) gingerbread man cookie cutter

110g (scant ¾ cup) plain (all-purpose) flour + extra for dusting
½ tsp bicarbonate of soda (baking soda)
Pinch of salt
1 tsp ground ginger
1 tsp ground cinnamon
⅛ tsp ground cloves
35g (1.25oz) unsalted butter, softened
40g (3 tbsp) light or brown sugar
40ml (3 tbsp) treacle (molasses)
½ small egg (see page 19)
¼ tsp vanilla extract

TO DECORATE:
White icing pen
Red and green festive decorations

01 In a medium bowl, mix together the flour, bicarbonate of soda (baking soda), salt, ginger, cinnamon and cloves until combined, then set aside.

02 In a medium-large bowl, using an electric hand mixer, beat the butter until creamy, then add the sugar and treacle (molasses) and beat until fully combined and creamy. Beat in the egg and vanilla extract, scraping down the sides of the bowl as needed. Don't worry if the butter separates.

03 Pour the flour mixture into the wet ingredients and fold in using a rubber spatula or wooden spoon until combined. The dough should be thick and slightly sticky.

04 Roll the dough into a disc, then wrap in cling film (plastic wrap) and chill in the refrigerator for at least 3 hours. Chilling is a must for this recipe.

05 Remove your gingerbread dough from the refrigerator. Flour your surface, your hands and your rolling pin. Roll the dough to 5mm (¼in) thick. If the dough cracks as you roll it, just push it back together and keep lifting and rotating the dough to help.

06 Preheat the air fryer to 150°C (300°F).

07 Cut out 6 gingerbread men. Line the air fryer rack or basket with a sheet of thick baking paper. Place 2.5cm (1in) apart on the baking paper and bake for 8–10 minutes. If some of the cookies look like they're cooking quicker than others, rotate the positioning so they cook evenly. Leave to cool for 5 minutes on the baking paper, then remove them to cool completely.

TO DECORATE:

08 Decorate however you wish. I like to use a white icing pen and some little red and green festive decorations.

09 Store in an airtight container at room temperature for up to 5 days.

NOT-GINGERBREAD MEN

Makes 4

This is for everyone out there who doesn't like gingerbread but still wants to make gingerbread men for Christmas. This chocolate pastry version is so quick and easy to make and is guaranteed to please just about anyone.

35 minutes

SPECIAL EQUIPMENT:
10cm (4in) gingerbread man cookie cutter

1 sheet ready-rolled puff pastry
75g (4 tbsp) chocolate hazelnut spread (I use Nutella)
1 small egg + 1 tsp milk or water, for the egg wash
Granulated sugar, for sprinkling (optional)
Icing (powdered) sugar, for dusting (optional)

01 Unravel the puff pastry and lay it out in a landscape position, then spread the chocolate hazelnut spread over one half of the pastry and fold in half so the spread is covered (like you are closing a book).

02 Use the cookie cutter to cut out 4 shapes (or more if you can). Seal the edges with the back of a fork and prick the tops.

03 Make your egg wash by beating the egg with the milk or in a small bowl, then brush it over the top of the pastries. Sprinkle the tops with a little granulated sugar if you wish.

04 Preheat the air fryer to 180°C (350°F).

05 Place a sheet of thick baking paper in the air fryer, then carefully transfer the shapes onto the baking paper at least 3cm (1¼in) apart. Air fry for 10–12 minutes until the pastry is crisp and golden brown. You may need to bake them in a few batches, depending on the size of your air fryer.

06 Remove the pastries from the air fryer and leave to cool slightly, then dust them with icing (powdered) sugar, if you like, and they're ready to eat. Best served fresh on the day. Enjoy!

Swap the chocolate hazelnut spread for any spread of your choice to change up the flavour.

INDEX

A
air fryer s'mores 91
air fryers
  buttons/functions 11
  checking food is done 10
  cleaning 15
  equipment 16
  getting to know yours 10
  how they work 10
  metric vs imperial measurements 14
  mistakes 14
  oven times vs air fryer cooking times 12–13
  overcrowding 14
  preheating 11
  size 11
  tips and tricks 14–15
  types of 11
apples
  blooming apples 88
  cinnamon apple chips 94
  speculoos apple crumble 204
  upside down apple Danish 48
apricots: flapjack bites 92

B
bacon
  bacon and cheese quesadilla 36
  barbecue chicken and cheese wrap 118
  Brie, bacon and mango chutney panini 120
  festive 'leftovers' toastie 240
  hunter's chicken 149
  loaded cubed potatoes 83
  loaded potato skins 62
  pigs in blankets with honey mustard glaze 234
  sausage and bacon French toast rolls 34
bagel bites, pizza 80
baked beans
  egg, bean and cheese breakfast pot 26
  loaded baked potato 76
  savoury French toast bake 32

bakes
  chicken fajita bakes 112
  savoury French toast bake 32
  speculoos French toast bake 39
bananas
  banana bread 208
  stuffed banana muffins 188
barbecue chicken and cheese wrap 118
barbecue chicken nachos 64
barbecue chicken wings 60
beans
  egg, bean and cheese breakfast pot 26
  loaded baked potato 76
  savoury French toast bake 32
beef
  beef Bolognese 146
  crunch wrap 107
  loaded baked potato 76
  stuffed peppers 150
berry crumble 192
biscuits see cookies and biscuits
blondies, white chocolate 160
blooming apples 88
blueberry pancakes 40
Bolognese, beef 146
bread
  baked Camembert 242
  Brie, bacon and mango chutney panini 120
  cheesy stuffed garlic bread sticks 70
  chocolate toast pies 55
  festive 'leftovers' toastie 240
  ham and cheese toastie 116
  peri-peri chicken burger 126
  pizza pockets 67
  pizza toastie 100
  prawn toast 72
  sausage and bacon French toast rolls 34
  savoury French toast bake 32
  speculoos French toast bake 39
Brie, bacon and mango chutney panini 120
brioche French toast, stuffed 44

broccoli: veggie noodle stir-fry 130
brownies, fudgy 158
buffalo cauliflower 75
buns: French toast bites 50
burgers, peri-peri chicken 126
burritos
  chicken burrito 104
  veggie breakfast burrito 24
buttercream
  funfetti cake 184
  mini confetti cakes 200
  sprinkle cookie sandwiches 168–9
  vanilla cupcakes 215

C
cabbage: tropical shrimp tacos 144
Cajun-spiced salmon bites 110
cakes
  banana bread 208
  chocolate lava cakes 187
  fudgy brownies 158
  funfetti cake 184
  mini confetti cakes 200
  mini cookies and cream cakes 194
  mini speculoos cakes 207
  peanut butter lava cakes 199
  vanilla cupcakes 215
  white chocolate blondies 160
Camembert, baked 242
caramel oat cookie bars 174
carrots: veggie noodle stir-fry 130
cauliflower, buffalo 75
cheat's marinara sauce 142
cheese
  bacon and cheese quesadilla 36
  baked Camembert 242
  barbecue chicken and cheese wrap 118
  barbecue chicken nachos 64
  cheese twists 84
  cheesy stuffed garlic bread sticks 70
  chicken parm 142
  crunch wrap 107

egg, bean and cheese breakfast pot 26
ham and cheese toastie 116
hunter's chicken 149
loaded baked potato 76
loaded cubed potatoes 83
loaded hash browns 28
loaded potato skins 62
mac 'n' cheese 128
naan pizza 115
peri-peri chicken burger 126
pizza bagel bites 80
pizza pockets 67
pizza toastie 100
sausage and bacon French toast rolls 34
savoury French toast bake 32
shakshuka 31
stuffed crust pizza 133
stuffed peppers 150
tomato gnocchi 134
veggie breakfast burrito 24
veggie pastry slices 108
cheesecakes, baked white chocolate mini 196
chicken
　barbecue chicken and cheese wrap 118
　barbecue chicken nachos 64
　barbecue chicken wings 60
　chicken burrito 104
　chicken fajita bakes 112
　chicken parm 142
　chicken tender tacos 136
　hot honey chicken tenders 102
　hunter's chicken 149
　loaded baked potato 76
　naan pizza 115
　peri-peri chicken burger 126
chips, cinnamon apple 94
chocolate
　air fryer s'mores 91
　baked white chocolate mini cheesecakes 196
　banana bread 208
　caramel oat cookie bars 174
　choc chip shortbread cookie sandwiches 164
　chocolate chip cookie baked oats 42
　chocolate egg lava pots 226
　chocolate lava cakes 187
　chocolate toast pies 55
　double chocolate shortbread cookies 172
　fudgy brownies 158
　melting chocolate 19
　mini chocolate egg cookie pots 229
　mini cookies and cream cakes 194
　mini scones 86
　mini triple chocolate cookies 176
　peanut butter lava cakes 199
　skillet cookie 171
　soft choc chip cookies 156
　speculoos magic bars 166
　sprinkle cookie sandwiches 168–9
　stuffed banana muffins 188
　stuffed brioche French toast 44
　stuffed cookie pots 163
　thick NYC cookies 179
　white chocolate blondies 160
chocolate eggs
　chocolate egg lava pots 226
　mini chocolate egg cookie pots 229
chocolate hazelnut spread
　choc chip shortbread cookie sandwiches 164
　chocolate and strawberry pastry hearts 222
　chocolate hazelnut soufflés 212
　chocolate toast pies 55
　double chocolate shortbread cookies 172
　Easter bunny puff pastries 224
　mini s'mores pies 216
　not-gingerbread men 246
cinnamon
　blooming apples 88
　cinnamon apple chips 94
　cinnamon pastry swirls 52
　cinnamon roll granola 47
　puff pastry 'cronuts' 202
cobbler, peach 210
coconut shrimp 78
condensed milk: speculoos magic bars 166
confetti cakes, mini 200
cookie bars, caramel oat 174
cookie pots, mini chocolate egg 229
cookie sandwiches
　choc chip shortbread cookie sandwiches 164
　sprinkle cookie sandwiches 168–9
cookies and biscuits
　double chocolate shortbread cookies 172
　gingerbread men 245
　Halloween boo-biscuits 232–3
　mini triple chocolate cookies 176
　skillet cookie 171
　soft choc chip cookies 156
　stuffed cookie pots 163
　thick NYC cookies 179
cookies and cream biscuits: mini cookies and cream cakes 194
cornflakes
　chicken tender tacos 136
　hot honey chicken tenders 102
courgettes (zucchini): veggie pastry slices 108
cranberries: flapjack bites 92
cranberry sauce
　festive 'leftovers' toastie 240
　festive sausage rolls 238
cream
　baked white chocolate mini cheesecakes 196
　chocolate and strawberry pastry hearts 222
　Easter bunny puff pastries 224
cream cheese
　baked white chocolate mini cheesecakes 196
　cream cheese frosting 188
'cronuts', puff pastry 202
crumbles
　berry crumble 192
　speculoos apple crumble 204
crunch wrap 107
cupcakes, vanilla 215

D
Danish, upside down apple 48
digestive biscuits
　air fryer s'mores 91
　baked white chocolate mini cheesecakes 196
　mini s'mores pies 216
double chocolate shortbread cookies 172
dried fruit: flapjack bites 92

E
Easter bunny puff pastries 224
eggs 19
　bacon and cheese quesadilla 36

egg, bean and cheese breakfast pot 26
French toast bites 50
sausage and bacon French toast rolls 34
savoury French toast bake 32
shakshuka 31
speculoos French toast bake 39
stuffed brioche French toast 44
veggie breakfast burrito 24
equipment 16

F
fajita seasoning
  chicken burrito 104
  chicken fajita bakes 112
festive 'leftovers' toastie 240
festive sausage rolls 238
fish
  Cajun-spiced salmon bites 110
  loaded baked potato 76
  teriyaki salmon 138
flapjack bites 92
French toast
  French toast bites 50
  sausage and bacon French toast rolls 34
  savoury French toast bake 32
  speculoos French toast bake 39
  stuffed brioche French toast 44
fries, sweet potato 68
frostings
  buttercream 168–9, 184, 200, 215
  cream cheese frosting 188
fudgy brownies 158
funfetti cake 184

G
garlic bread sticks, cheesy stuffed 70
gingerbread men 245
  not-gingerbread men 246
gnocchi, tomato 134
granola, cinnamon roll 47
green beans: veggie noodle stir-fry 130

H
halloumi cheese: peri-peri chicken burger 126
Halloween boo-biscuits 232–3
ham
  ham and cheese toastie 116
  naan pizza 115

hash browns, loaded 28
honey
  hot honey chicken tenders 102
  pigs in blankets with honey mustard glaze 234
  upside down apple Danish 48
hunter's chicken 149

I
ingredients 19

J
jam: mini pastry pies 191

L
lava cakes
  chocolate lava cakes 187
  peanut butter lava cakes 199
lava pots, chocolate egg 226
'leftovers' toastie, festive 240
lettuce
  crunch wrap 107
  peri-peri chicken burger 126
loaded baked potato 76
loaded cubed potatoes 83
loaded hash browns 28
loaded potato skins 62

M
mac 'n' cheese 128
magic bars, speculoos 166
mango: tropical shrimp tacos 144
mango chutney: Brie, bacon and mango chutney panini 120
maple syrup: blueberry pancakes 40
marshmallows
  air fryer s'mores 91
  mini s'mores pies 216
muffins, stuffed banana 188
mummy dogs 230
mustard: pigs in blankets with honey mustard glaze 234

N
naan pizza 115
nachos, barbecue chicken 64
noodles: veggie noodle stir-fry 130
not-gingerbread men 246
Nutella see chocolate hazelnut spread
nuts: flapjack bites 92

O
oats
  caramel oat cookie bars 174
  chocolate chip cookie baked oats 42
  cinnamon roll granola 47
  flapjack bites 92
oils/cooking sprays 15

P
pancakes, blueberry 40
panini, Brie, bacon and mango chutney 120
panko breadcrumbs
  buffalo cauliflower 75
  chicken parm 142
  coconut shrimp 78
paprika
  buffalo cauliflower 75
  chicken tender tacos 136
pasta
  beef Bolognese 146
  mac 'n' cheese 128
  veggie noodle stir-fry 130
pastry hearts, chocolate and strawberry 222
peach cobbler 210
peanut butter lava cakes 199
pecans: flapjack bites 92
pepperoni
  naan pizza 115
  pizza bagel bites 80
  pizza pockets 67
  pizza toastie 100
peppers
  chicken burrito 104
  chicken fajita bakes 112
  shakshuka 31
  stuffed peppers 150
  tomato gnocchi 134
  veggie noodle stir-fry 130
  veggie pastry slices 108
peri-peri chicken burger 126
pesto: veggie pastry slices 108
pies
  mini pastry pies 191
  mini s'mores pies 216
pigs in blankets
  festive 'leftovers' toastie 240
  pigs in blankets with honey mustard glaze 234
pizza
  naan pizza 115
  pizza bagel bites 80
  pizza pockets 67

pizza toastie 100
stuffed crust pizza 133
pizza sauce
  cheat's marinara sauce 142
  loaded baked potato 76
  naan pizza 115
  pizza bagel bites 80
  pizza pockets 67
  pizza toastie 100
  stuffed crust pizza 133
potatoes
  loaded baked potato 76
  loaded cubed potatoes 83
  loaded hash browns 28
  loaded potato skins 62
prawns *see* shrimp/prawns
puff pastry
  cheese twists 84
  chicken fajita bakes 112
  chocolate and strawberry pastry hearts 222
  cinnamon pastry swirls 52
  Easter bunny puff pastries 224
  festive sausage rolls 238
  mummy dogs 230
  not-gingerbread men 246
  puff pastry 'cronuts' 202
  upside down apple Danish 48
  veggie pastry slices 108
puffed rice cereal: cinnamon roll granola 47

Q
quesadilla, bacon and cheese 36

R
raisins: mini scones 86
rice: chicken burrito 104

S
salmon
  Cajun-spiced salmon bites 110
  teriyaki salmon 138
salted caramel sauce: caramel oat cookie bars 174
sausages
  festive 'leftovers' toastie 240
  festive sausage rolls 238
  mummy dogs 230
  pigs in blankets with honey mustard glaze 234
  sausage and bacon French toast rolls 34
  toad in the hole 141
savoury French toast bake 32

scones, mini 86
sesame seeds: prawn toast 72
shakshuka 31
shortbread cookies
  choc chip shortbread cookie sandwiches 164
  double chocolate shortbread cookies 172
shortcrust pastry: mini pastry pies 191
shrimp/prawns
  coconut shrimp 78
  loaded baked potato 76
  prawn toast 72
  tropical shrimp tacos 144
skillet cookie 171
s'mores
  air fryer s'mores 91
  mini s'mores pies 216
soft choc chip cookies 156
soufflés, chocolate hazelnut 212
speculoos biscuits: speculoos magic bars 166
speculoos spread
  mini speculoos cakes 207
  speculoos apple crumble 204
  speculoos French toast bake 39
sprinkle cookie sandwiches 168–9
sprinkles 19
stir-fry, veggie noodle 130
strawberries: chocolate and strawberry pastry hearts 222
stuffed banana muffins 188
stuffed brioche French toast 44
stuffed cookie pots 163
stuffed crust pizza 133
stuffed peppers 150
stuffing: festive 'leftovers' toastie 240
sunflower seeds: flapjack bites 92
sweet potato fries 68
sweetcorn: loaded baked potato 76

T
tacos
  chicken tender tacos 136
  tropical shrimp tacos 144
teriyaki salmon 138
thick NYC cookies 179
toad in the hole 141
toasties
  festive 'leftovers' toastie 240

ham and cheese toastie 116
  pizza toastie 100
  tomato and mascarpone sauce: ham and cheese toastie 116
tomatoes
  barbecue chicken nachos 64
  beef Bolognese 146
  chicken burrito 104
  peri-peri chicken burger 126
  shakshuka 31
  stuffed peppers 150
  tomato gnocchi 134
  veggie pastry slices 108
tortilla chips
  barbecue chicken nachos 64
  crunch wrap 107
tortilla wraps
  bacon and cheese quesadilla 36
  barbecue chicken and cheese wrap 118
  chicken burrito 104
  chicken tender tacos 136
  crunch wrap 107
  tropical shrimp tacos 144
  veggie breakfast burrito 24
tropical shrimp tacos 144
tuna: loaded baked potato 76
turkey: festive 'leftovers' toastie 240

U
upside down apple Danish 48

V
vanilla cupcakes 215
veggie breakfast burrito 24
veggie noodle stir-fry 130
veggie pastry slices 108

W
white chocolate blondies 160
wraps
  barbecue chicken and cheese wrap 118
  crunch wrap 107
  see also tortilla wraps

Y
yogurt
  blueberry pancakes 40
  chocolate chip cookie baked oats 42
Yorkshire puddings 237

CONVERSION TABLES

MEASUREMENTS

Metric	Imperial
5mm	¼ inch
1cm	½ inch
1.5cm	⅝ inch
2cm	¾ inch
2.5cm	1 inch
3cm	1¼ inch
4cm	1½ inch
5cm	2 inches
7.5cm	3 inches
10cm	4 inches
15cm	6 inches
19cm	7½ inches

OVEN TEMPERATURES

°C	Fan °C	°F	Gas Mark
140°C	120°C	275°F	Gas Mark 1
150°C	130°C	300°F	Gas Mark 2
160°C	140°C	325°F	Gas Mark 3
180°C	160°C	350°F	Gas Mark 4
190°C	170°C	375°F	Gas Mark 5
200°C	180°C	400°F	Gas Mark 6
220°C	200°C	425°F	Gas Mark 7
230°C	210°C	450°F	Gas Mark 8
240°C	220°C	475°F	Gas Mark 9

WEIGHTS	
Metric	Imperial
10g	½ oz
25g	1 oz
40g	1½ oz
60g	2 oz
90g	3 oz
115g	4 oz
150g	5¼ oz
175g	6 oz
200g	7 oz
225g	8 oz
250g	9 oz
275g	10 oz
330g	12 oz
375g	13 oz
400g	14 oz
450g	15 oz
500g	1 lb
550g	1¼ lb
600g	1½ lb
900g	2 lb
1.5kg	3 lb
1.75kg	4 lb
2.25kg	5 lb

VOLUME	
Metric	Imperial
25ml	1 fl oz
50ml	2 fl oz
85ml	3 fl oz
150ml	5 fl oz (¼ pint)
300ml	10 fl oz (½ pint)
450ml	15 fl oz (¾ pint)
600ml	1 pint
700ml	1¼ pints
900ml	1½ pints
1 litre	1¾ pints
1.2 litres	2 pints
1.25 litres	2¼ pints
1.5 litres	2½ pints
1.6 litres	2¾ pints
1.75 litres	3 pints
1.8 litres	3¼ pints
2 litres	3½ pints
2.1 litres	3¾ pints
2.25 litres	4 pints
2.75 litres	5 pints
3.4 litres	6 pints
3.9 litres	7 pints
5 litres	8 pints (1 gal)

ACKNOWLEDGEMENTS

Creating a book is something I couldn't do alone. It's a year-long project that has so much work going into it from every angle, so I want to say thank you to every single person who made this book possible. First, I want to give a special mention to my online community and audience, because without your continuous love and support, I wouldn't have had the opportunity to write a book in the first place, let alone a fourth book! Every time I get to meet you guys in person it fills my heart with so much joy, I think it could explode. You guys are the best!

Thank you to the amazing team who made this book come to life and look so incredible. Thank you to Faith Mason for your beautiful photography throughout the book. Thank you to Katie Marshall and her team for being the best food stylists ever – you make the food looks so perfect and delicious every single time. Thank you to Daisy Shayler-Webb for styling the most amazing colourful props around each dish. The amount of work that goes into each photo is so impressive, and I absolutely love working with you all.

Thank you to Studio Nic&Lou for the gorgeous designs, colours, patterns and for making this book as beautiful as it is. You always manage to capture everything I love on paper and make the book so special.

Thank you to my brilliant editor Emily Brickell from Ebury Press for being the glue that holds everything together. We are so lucky to have you as our editor.

Thank you to my wonderful literary agents, Eve, Ludo and Steven, who continue to help and support me every step of the way. Four years ago, Eve came to me and asked if I wanted to write a book, helped me write a book proposal and the rest was history. I cannot thank you all enough.

Thank you to Holly and Jon for coming into my natural habitat (my kitchen) and capturing all my best angles. You make me feel so comfortable and you're an absolute pleasure to work with.

Finally, thank you to Bernie, my magnificent husband, the chief taste tester, number one supporter, admin assistant, professional comforter, cake inspector and all-round genius. Fitwaffle wouldn't be what it is without you.

Love Eloise x

Ebury Press

UK | USA | Canada | Ireland | Australia
India | New Zealand | South Africa

Ebury Press is part of the Penguin Random House group of companies whose addresses can be found at global.penguinrandomhouse.com

Penguin Random House UK
One Embassy Gardens, 8 Viaduct Gardens, London SW11 7BW

penguin.co.uk
global.penguinrandomhouse.com

First published by Ebury Press in 2025

2

Copyright © Eloise Head 2025
Photography © Faith Mason except pages 9, 18 and 255
Photography on pages 9, 18 and 255 © Holly Pickering

The moral right of the author has been asserted.

No part of this book may be used or reproduced in any manner for the purpose of training artificial intelligence technologies or systems. In accordance with Article 4(3) of the DSM Directive 2019/790, Penguin Random House expressly reserves this work from the text and data mining exception.

Senior Editor: Emily Brickell
Senior Production Manager: Lucy Harrison
Design: Studio Nic&Lou
Photography: Faith Mason
Food Stylist: Katie Marshall
Prop Stylist: Daisy Shayler-Webb

Colour origination by Altaimage Ltd
Printed and bound in Germany by Mohn Media

The authorised representative in the EEA is Penguin Random House Ireland, Morrison Chambers, 32 Nassau Street, Dublin D02 YH68.

A CIP catalogue record for this book is available from the British Library

ISBN 9781529947304

Penguin Random House is committed to a sustainable future for our business, our readers and our planet. This book is made from Forest Stewardship Council® certified paper

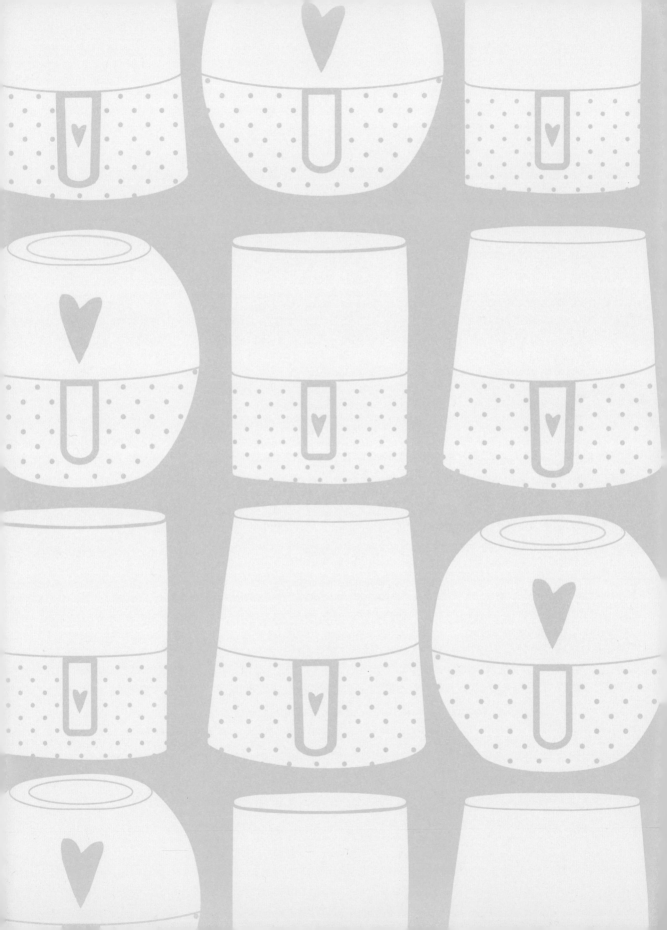